FAT CAT THIN

D1122808

FAT CAT THIN

David Alderton

Northern Plains Public Library
Ault Colorado

hamlyn

An Hachette Livre UK Company

First published in Great Britain in 2007 by
Hamlyn, a division of Octopus Publishing Group Ltd
2–4 Heron Quays, London E14 4JP
www.octopusbooks.co.uk

Distributed in the United States and Canada by
Sterling Publishing Co., Inc.
387 Park Avenue South, New York, NY 10016-8810

Copyright © Octopus Publishing Group Ltd 2007

All rights reserved. No part of this work may be reproduced or utilized in any form
or by any means, electronic or mechanical, including photocopying, recording or
by any information storage and retrieval system, without the prior written permission
of the publisher.

ISBN-13: 978-0-600-61653-5
ISBN-10: 0-600-61653-3

A CIP catalogue record for this book is available from the British Library

Printed and bound in China
10 9 8 7 6 5 4 3 2

Note
This book is not intended as a substitute for veterinary advice and you should
consult your vet if you think your cat may be suffering from obesity.

Contents

Introduction

One of the most appealing things about cats is their natural athletic grace and elegance. If, however, you allow your cat to become overweight through overfeeding or lack of exercise, these characteristic features will be lost and perhaps even more significantly, your pet's personality will be affected too. Your cat is likely to display less interest in life and will sleep for longer periods each day as well. This can mark the start of a downward spiral, where your cat begins taking less exercise and gains more weight as a consequence. In turn, the risk of your pet dying prematurely will be significantly raised at a stage when, ironically, the life expectancy of cats generally is increasing.

The good news is that once you are alert to the signs of unwanted weight gain, you can prevent the situation arising. Also, if you have a cat that is already overweight, you can follow the steps in this book to slim your pet down and to improve its overall health as well. The sooner you act, the easier it will be to achieve these goals.

Although the number of overweight cats is rising dramatically according to veterinary surveys, there is no reason why your cat should join this group – particularly as cats are not naturally prone to

obesity. This book highlights the key risk factors for weight gain, so if you are starting out with a young kitten it should also serve as a guide to ensure that your pet remains in peak condition for life.

Much of the recent rise in feline obesity is due to lifestyle changes that we have imposed on our pets – not letting them wander outdoors freely for fear of traffic, for example, or to prevent risk of injury caused by fighting with other cats in the neighbourhood. Kept inside in the warm, with little to do other than eat in many cases, it is not surprising that the level of obesity amongst the cat population has risen so dramatically.

Although cats can start to gain excess weight at only a few months old, they are more vulnerable to obesity in the later years of life. This is partly because their activity levels decline with age while their calorie input often remains constant. Getting your cat to lose weight successfully depends not only on altering the quantity or type of food that it is eating, but also on increasing your pet's level of activity to burn off unwanted body fat. The playful nature of cats should help you to encourage your pet to become more active again, and there are a number of suggestions in the following pages about how this can be achieved at any age.

Domesticated Hunters

Cats have independent natures. They may choose to associate with humans, but it is quite clear that they can survive on their own, as shown by the populations of feral cats living in virtually all major cities of the world. Secretive by nature, these cats often conceal their presence, choosing locations that offer some privacy from people, such as docks, industrial sites and overgrown railway embankments. They live in places as varied as vacant buildings and burrows made by other animals.

In such localities, the cats can hunt rodents for food, as well as birds such as pigeons. If prey becomes scarce, the cats may wander farther afield to scavenge the streets for leftovers from the human population. These feral colonies are the result of abandoned or stray domestic cats that have been forced to live wild and find their own food. They manage not only to survive, but also to breed and rear kittens. Life in such surroundings is harsh, though, and few feral cats have a lifespan approaching that of a beloved household pet.

In many ways, feral cats are living in a similar way to cats that existed before the domestication process began, possibly 8,000 years ago. It would seem that people did not actively seek the company of cats, but rather that cats were attracted to humans, because our lifestyle guaranteed them a source of food. Since the days of ancient Egypt, cats have benefited from association with people, and have been welcomed as a means of controlling vermin. The presence of rodents near grain and other food stores served to draw African Wild Cats into ancient Egyptian settlements. Before long, cats were encouraged to live alongside humans due to their 'pest control' habits.

As anyone who has ever tried to cuddle a cat who is 'not in the mood' will realize, a cat cannot be forced into anything. It is out of choice that they return to their owners – often for food, as well as for shelter and companionship – so it is in our interests to provide them with the safe domestic setting and healthy lifestyle that these graceful creatures deserve.

Independent in nature, domestic cats are, nevertheless, dependent on their owners to provide a healthy balanced diet.

Wild Cat Hunters

In the wild, cats spend much of their time seeking food. They are well equipped for this task, possessing keen senses, excellent co-ordination and the ability to kill prey efficiently. Wild cats, especially the smaller species, tend to be more active after the hours of darkness, which is also when rodents are most likely to emerge from their hiding places. Cats can display great patience and concentration, waiting for lengthy periods of time near places such as rabbit burrows for their quarry to venture out. On the other hand, many larger cats actively stalk prey, waiting for their target to come within reach before launching a strike.

This strategy is evident in the case of the Cheetah, which is the fastest land mammal on the planet, able to run at speeds equivalent to 100 kph (62 mph). The Cheetah attempts to move undetected as close to its target as possible, before unleashing its deadly pace in pursuit of

Keen eyesight is a feature of all cats, allowing them to pinpoint with great accuracy where to strike. This is achieved by binocular vision, which effectively gives a three-dimensional view of their prey directly in front of them. The images from each eye overlap to an extent, allowing the cat's brain to interpret the prey's position precisely, ready for strike.

All the cat's senses are finely tuned – a cat can even hear high-frequency sounds that are completely inaudible to human ears. This allows cats to detect rodents in an area where we may not know they are present. Some cats, such as the Serval, rely heavily on their hearing for this purpose, hunting rodents in grassland areas where they are far from conspicuous. This particular wild cat has large ears, which allow it to trap sound waves efficiently and assist in accurately locating their source.

Quite apart from its speed, other aspects of the cat's athletic nature help it to catch prey. A number of smaller species can jump well, and also climb. The Caracal Lynx is able to leap so effectively that it can use its paws to knock down birds flushed out of grassland areas in mid-flight. Other small wild cats, such as the Margay, actually hunt birds in the trees. They are very agile, with their keen vision enabling them to jump safely from branch to branch without falling. Even if a cat does slip and lose its grip, its co-ordination is such that it can swivel its body around almost instantaneously and land on its feet, minimizing the risk of injury in the event of a fall.

Athleticism is key to a cat's survival in the wild. The Cheetah is famous for its ability to run with immense speed over short distances.

its prey. Adapted for sprinting rather than a long-distance pursuit, the Cheetah remains hidden from its quarry until the last moment because this dramatically increases the likelihood that it will be able to make a kill.

Harsh Lessons in Survival

Although popularly perceived as predators, life can be as harsh for wild cats as it is for their prey. Their hunting ability is part instinctive and part acquired, with the female, who rears her cubs on her own, educating her young in how to hunt successfully.

Not all master this training, however. Cheetah cubs suffer a high rate of mortality in the period immediately after weaning, simply because they cannot capture prey. Being young, they do not yet possess the blistering pace of an adult Cheetah, and this places more demands on their hunting skills while they are still relatively inexperienced. This is a critical phase in a Cheetah's life. If it cannot make a kill, the young Cheetah will grow weak, and will ultimately starve.

The difference between survival and death is therefore finely balanced, even for dominant predators like Cheetahs and other big cats. Anything that is a handicap to hunting represents a serious threat, even pregnancy. The increase in weight at this stage slows down the female Cheetah's ability to run, so she is likely to have difficulty pursuing prey. Evolution has tried to cope with this, as cats generally do not put on a significant amount of weight until the end of their pregnancy. The embryo's body differentiates initially, giving rise to the body organs, but with the growth in size being the final phase prior to birth. This further emphasizes the cat's natural reliance on speed and athleticism to survive.

Dangers of Hunting

Hunting is a potentially dangerous pastime in any event, and a Cheetah's life can easily be cut short by injury because it relies so heavily on its pace to obtain its prey. While a minor injury may not be fatal, it could easily condemn a cat to a slow death through starvation. The majority of wild cats depend on their individual hunting abilities to catch their quarry, with only lions hunting in groups. This task is undertaken by the lionesses in the pride working collaboratively, without the male. Even fierce hunters such as tigers or jaguars sometimes come off worse in encounters with their prey, leaving them crippled or even dead as

the result of an ill-judged leap or a blow from an animal's hooves or horns.

Smaller wild cats face an equally precarious existence. Studies show that even proficient hunters have a low return based on the strikes that they make, with prey often eluding them. They may only be successful once in four or more attempts. Anything that can tilt the balance even slightly in their favour is therefore of value. While cheetahs and other large cats are adept at

Cheetah cubs (below) face starvation if they are unsuccessful when hunting; tigers (right) are especially adapted to harsh cold climates.

targeting a weakened or young individual in a herd, smaller species tend to seek fledglings in order to give themselves an advantage. Young birds that have only recently left the nest, for example, will not yet have acquired the awareness and fast reaction times of adult birds.

The lifestyle of wild cats therefore means they are unlikely to be overweight. They have to be fit and in peak condition to survive. Even so, they frequently die prematurely in the wild, because of the many dangers that they face and their lack of success in obtaining food.

Dealing With Prey

A cat that has been reared in a cattery without ever seeing natural prey will still develop an interest in hunting, although it is less likely to be successful, especially without its mother's instruction. It is crucial, however, for a wild cat to be able to kill prey quickly, to prevent the prey from struggling free and possibly injuring the cat. Most cats use the long canine teeth at the corners of their mouth to kill prey, sinking these teeth through the neck of the victim to sever the spinal cord; cheetahs grab the throat of their prey to suffocate it. A cat's teeth slide into place very effectively, so as to prevent them from biting into the bone of the vertebral column and breaking. Deprived of this means of killing its quarry, a wild cat could easily face starvation.

Adaptable Predators

Wild cats are unlikely to suffer from obesity, and the same is true of domestic cats that revert to a feral lifestyle. It is clear that we are responsible for the increase in obesity among our pets. Veering far from the wild cat's natural diet and lifestyle, we have lost sight of the fact that our pets share the traits and requirements of their wild relatives.

Domestic cats, especially when they revert to a free-living or feral lifestyle, will target a wide range of prey. Where they have been introduced in Australia and New Zealand, for example, they have preyed on slow-moving marsupials. Abandoned on islands, cats left by sailing ships in the past have tended to become the dominant predators, even to the extent of eliminating various birds, particularly nesting colonies of seabirds. This happened on Herekopare Island off New Zealand, where Broad-Billed Prions and the Diving Petrel were wiped out in barely half a century.

Feral cats have much stronger hunting instincts than household cats, because they must rely on these skills for survival. Queens with litters of

kittens are especially adept and enthusiastic hunters. The feeding preferences of young cats can be set very early in life; kittens that were reared primarily on mice, for example, rarely hunt rabbits or even rats once they themselves become independent.

The most dramatic impact of the hunting preferences and abilities of a population of feral cats in recent times was seen on the Turks and Caicos Islands in the Caribbean – a population of more than 15,000 native iguanas was wiped out within four years of the arrival of the cats, in 1974, largely as a result of the cats' aggressive hunting.

There is a difference in size between the sexes of feral cats, with the result that mature tom cats

The urge to hunt is a strong instinct even in domestic cats, which will rarely eat their kills.

tend to take larger prey such as rabbits, whereas queens will feed to a greater extent on mice and voles. Cats cannot dig below ground to flush out their quarry; they must wait to seize prey when it emerges from underground. Young rabbits are targeted in particular, because they are smaller, and they also tend to be less wary than adults. Invertebrates such as butterflies can also feature in the diets of young wild cats, because they are relatively easy to catch compared with other prey.

Domestic Cats and Hunting

One of the most distressing things for cat lovers is the way in which their pets continue to hunt in spite of being well fed. This can be explained by the behaviour of their wild ancestors. Some bigger cats, such as lions, gorge themselves after a kill; leopards, on the other hand, hide the remains of their prey up a tree so that they can return to feed at a later stage. African Wild Cats, from which most domestic cats descend, are constantly on the search for food. This is because they take relatively small prey, such as mice, which are swallowed whole. They therefore need to make more kills if they are not to go hungry.

The instinct to search for food does not necessarily mean that a cat is hungry, but when food is plentiful, cats will take advantage of the situation. Swarms of locusts, for example, provide easy hunting opportunities for wild cats, allowing a cat to feed almost at will, while domestic cats have been known to consume as many as a dozen mice at a time.

Catching wild prey is not a significant contributory factor in the development of feline obesity in domestic cats; in many cases, the prey is not actually eaten. Domestication of the cat may actually have enhanced their desire to hunt, though, since some cats will bring a variety of prey into the home, intended for their owners. They do not attempt to eat this food, but simply deposit it, confirming that the desire to hunt is separate from the impulse to eat. This behaviour is most commonly noted in female cats, suggesting that it is allied with their powerful maternal instincts towards the family.

CAN CATS WIPE OUT RODENTS?

There is no real likelihood of cats wiping out entire populations of rodents, especially where there are high densities, and food for the rodents is abundant. However, cats can certainly help to keep the numbers of rodents in check, and this can be achieved even when the cats are receiving food from humans. The effectiveness of cats at controlling rats is most obvious when the rodents are breeding, because cats generally target the young rather than adult rats, which are more wary. At certain points in the year, however, cats may switch to hunting young rabbits or birds that can be caught more easily at that time, allowing the rodent population to swell once more.

One aspect of the behaviour of domestic cats has changed dramatically from that of their wild relatives: they are now much more active during the day than at night, and this may impact on their hunting techniques. Some individuals appear to have much stronger hunting desires than others, and can spend up to half the day seeking prey, whereas others show no interest in hunting whatsoever. However, all cats that are fed spend less time hunting than their feral counterparts because they are not dependent on this activity for food. The level of activity may influence whether a particular cat is prone to obesity or not.

As with wild cats, domestic breeds also exhibit differences in their hunting techniques. Relatively stocky breeds, such as British Shorthairs, favour hunting on the ground, whereas Orientals and Siamese, which are lighter in weight and more agile by nature, frequently climb into trees to raid nests. Cats also become more interested in hunting when prey is relatively abundant, and therefore easier to catch. This is because they do not need to hunt in order to obtain food – they do so because it is still instinctive to. During the spring, for example, when young birds are learning to fly, prey will be in abundance.

Stalking prey is done over long distances by wild cats, whereas domestic cats tend not to have the same patience as their relatives.

Domestic cats are also adaptable in their hunting technique. If you fit your cat with a collar (elasticated to prevent the cat from becoming caught on branches) and attach a bell to alert birds to the cat's presence, you are likely to find that this soon stops serving as a warning. Instead, your cat will modify its hunting technique, moving in a slow and deliberate fashion so that the bell does not ring until the very last minute, when the cat launches into a potentially lethal strike.

Although it is often said that only dogs can be trained, hunting is one aspect of a cat's behaviour that reveals that cats can also learn. Once kittens are about a month old, for example, the queen will start to bring live prey for them, encouraging them to kill the creatures. This ability to learn can be significant in addressing the issue of feline obesity. By altering your cat's behaviour, you can help to overcome the lifestyle issues that have contributed to its obesity.

Diet and Metabolism

Another significant reason why wild and feral cats are not prone to obesity relates to their food. They are carnivores, feeding on meat or fish. This food comprises protein and fat, not carbohydrate. A cat's metabolism enables it to convert these foodstuffs into carbohydrate to meet the cat's energy needs, but carbohydrate does not feature in the cat's natural diet.

This lack of carbohydrate means that cats are less at risk of becoming obese. Their natural feeding habits are similar to those espoused by the Atkins diet as a weight-loss programme for humans. This also means that cats, being obligate carnivores, unlike dogs, cannot be kept in good health on a vegetarian diet. The only vegetable matter that cats consume is likely to be in the digestive tract of their prey. When a domestic cat eats grass, it is not doing so as a source of nourishment, but rather as an emetic, usually to help vomit up a hairball lodged in the stomach.

From the start of the domestication process right up to the 20th century, cats existed mainly on what they could catch for themselves, in addition to being given leftovers of meat and fish by humans. This undoubtedly helped to keep them relatively healthy. It is only in recent times that feline obesity has become a significant problem. A cat's nutritional requirements are far more specific than those of a dog; although it is possible to keep a dog in good health by feeding it cat food, a cat that is being fed nothing other than dog food will suffer from nutritional deficiencies. The cat is likely to go blind because of a lack of the amino acid taurine in such a diet; dogs, on the other hand, can convert other ingredients in their food to meet their requirements for taurine.

When slimming your pet, it is therefore essential that you learn about your cat's nutritional requirements (see chapter 4) and meet these needs to ensure optimum health.

A Growing Problem

Almost everything about cats, from their lifestyles to their feeding preferences, suggests that they are unlikely to become seriously overweight. However, all the indications are that cats are becoming significantly heavier than in the past, and this is likely to have highly detrimental effects on their health and lifespan.

The reasons for this trend reside partly in our changing relationship with cats, and partly in the way our lifestyles have altered over the course of the past century. Unless owners realize that allowing their cats to become overweight is detrimental to their pets' well being, this situation is unlikely to improve. In addition, it is not always immediately evident that a cat is gaining weight, so it is important to be aware of the early signs of obesity. This will allow you to tackle the problem as soon as possible.

The origins of feline obesity can be traced back to the late 1800s, when cats were increasingly brought indoors as household companions. These household pets tended to be home-loving and less prone to wandering than free-ranging cats. The development of the different cat breeds at this time was significant in changing the general perceived lifestyle of a cat. Persian Longhairs, for example, became very popular in the early years of the show scene, but these were not free-roaming cats. Rather, they were kept and bred in catteries.

Cat Size

Although the differences are nowhere near as marked as in dogs, there are significant variations in size between different cat breeds. The smallest is the rare and diminutive Singapura, which typically weighs less than 2.7 kg (6 lb), while at the other extreme, the Maine Coon is one of the largest breeds of pure African Wild Cat descent, typically weighing 7 kg (15.5 lb). However, there is no link between breed size and obesity in cats, so there is no excuse to let a large cat become obese.

A cat's size is dependent on the origins of the individual breed. The Persian was a companion breed essentially created for its looks, whereas some breeds have evolved naturally under the

CLIMATE, WEIGHT AND COLOUR CHANGES

The appearance of Siamese and related cats such as the Burmese does not change significantly during the year, just as the temperature in the parts of the world they originate from does not change significantly. Nevertheless, the climate does have some visible effects. The characteristic 'pointed' appearance of Siamese and similar breeds is influenced directly by their environment. The points are the darker areas at the extremities – the nose, ears, feet and tail.

The extent of pigmentation at the points is temperature-dependent, with cats living in warmer climates having paler points, and cats living in cooler climates having darker points. This is because blood flow to, and hence the local temperature of, the extremities is increased in warm conditions. Cats living in relatively cool surroundings require more energy to maintain their body temperature than those living in the warm, so those with less contrast between body and point colour may be more vulnerable to obesity because the temperature is warmer.

The appearance of the points may also be an indicator that a cat is overweight, because an obese cat will have a layer of insulating fat that increases the temperature of the points, making them paler.

same type of selection pressures as wild cats. These include the Maine Coon, America's first breed of domestic cat, and the Norwegian Forest Cat. Both of these are primarily working breeds,

The Maine Coon is one of the largest domesticated breeds of cat that is descended from the African Wild Cat, the ancestor of most domestic cats.

bred for living on farmsteads where they could control rodent populations. They are naturally large, reflecting the fact that they developed in cold climates. Their coats reinforce the impression of size and bulk, particularly during the winter months when the coat is at its thickest. In spring, however, these cats lose the distinctive ruff of long fur around the neck and their coats become shorter, reflecting the change in climate at this time of year. So, although it may appear that they have lost weight, they have actually just shed much of their long coat.

Animals living in cold climates tend to be larger than their relatives found in tropical areas, to enable them to keep warm. A larger body retains more heat, so they have to expend less energy on keeping warm. This explains why the breeds that have evolved under semi-natural conditions in the far north of the world, such as the Norwegian Forest Cat, are generally more bulky than those that evolved in warmer climes, such as the Siamese, which originated in Thailand. Siamese have short, sleek coats that hug their bodies, and lack the dense undercoat common to long-coated breeds from northern areas. If kept in warm areas and well fed, these larger northern cats can easily become obese.

Breed Development

Today's Siamese cats have changed significantly in appearance since they first became known in the West during the 1880s. Contemporary descriptions and photographs from the 19th century show that early Siamese were stockier and had more rounded faces than today's Siamese, with a profile similar to that of the breed now known as the colourpoint shorthair. Influenced by the judging standard used in cat shows, breeders subsequently sought to create cats with more angular faces and a more lithe appearance. What constitutes an ideal body shape for a pure-bred cat is influenced directly by this show standard.

The Siamese is a breed with a long history, but there are other cats of much more recent origins. In fact, the number of cat breeds grew dramatically during the second half of the 20th century, and is now approaching 100 in total, although some are scarce and not recognized for show purposes. Although a number of mutations have arisen spontaneously in cat populations, the bulk of the new breeds was created deliberately by cross-breeding.

The most popular newcomer of recent years marks a radical departure in breeding policy, because it is the result of hybridization rather than a direct descendant of the African Wild Cat. The aim with the Bengal was to transfer the markings of the Asian Leopard Cat to a domestic cat bloodline. The Bengal breeding programme began in the United States in the 1960s, but it was not until the 1980s that these cats became more widely available. After the initial cross-breeding, it takes about four generations of matings with domestic cats before kittens lose their obvious wild cat instincts and show the attributes of their domestic relatives.

The unusual Bengal has become much desired in recent years, particularly in the United States.

As a result of the difference in size between wild and domestic cats, the Bengal is a large breed, and this needs to be reflected in its food intake. This is why it is important to know the target weight of your cat, rather than just feeding your pet whenever it wants food. The feeding instructions on cat food provide clear information on how much food is needed, based on the cat's size. Follow these, or you are likely to overfeed your cat in response to its requests, and before long your pet will gain weight.

Another cross-breed of wild and domestic cats is the Chausie, involving the Jungle Cat, although it is not as well known as the Bengal. During the 1980s, crosses between domestic cats and Servals, which also originate from Africa, were made. These have now created a relatively tall, long-legged cat known as the Savannah, which is again growing in popularity. All these so-called hybrid breeds are significantly heavier than ordinary domestic cats, because of their origins. Just as in the case of their wild cat ancestors, toms of these breeds are also bigger than queens. Both Chausies and Savannahs can weigh up to 11.3 kg (25 lb). Depending on the breed, male cats may require a little more food than queens.

Is Your Cat Overweight?

To judge the weight of your cat, you need to assess its overall body condition. Look at your pet both from above and from the side. When viewed from above, you should see a smooth but gradual increase in the width of the body as it extends down to the tail. If there are bulges on the sides of the body, the cat is likely to be overweight. When viewed from the side, the lower line of the cat's body between the legs should appear straight, and should not dip down towards the abdomen – a clear indication that it is overweight. In cases of extreme obesity, the lower line may extend downwards below the level of the elbow.

It can be hard to judge if a long-haired breed is overweight; however, by regularly monitoring your cat's weight you will pick up any significant increases.

ASSESSING YOUR CAT'S WEIGHT

Target weight
- The abdomen feels taut.
- There is a definite narrowing of the waist.
- The rib-cage is visible: it can be seen when viewed from above.

Overweight
- The abdomen is slack.
- The waist is not well-defined.
- There is a continuous widening, from shoulders to hips.

Obese
- The abdomen hangs down: in severe cases to the level of the elbow.
- The waist is not visible.
- Ribs and hips are covered in excess fat.

Assessing a cat's body condition is reasonably straightforward if your pet is short-haired and will co-operate, but it is much harder in the case of a long-coated cat because of the overlay of fur, particularly during the winter months when the coat is at its thickest. You will need to examine your pet carefully by running your hands lightly but firmly along the sides of the body. You should be able to feel the ribs just beneath the skin as slight bony prominences. Any clear-cut gaps would indicate that your pet is underweight; if you have difficulty in locating your cat's ribs, your pet is seriously overweight. It is easier for obesity to creep up unnoticed in the case of a long-coated cat, because the signs are less apparent. This is why it is important to keep a check on your pet's state of health as part of the regular grooming process. It will be much simpler to correct the problem if you spot it early before it becomes serious.

It is harder to determine whether a cat is overweight than it is a dog, particularly in the case of pure-bred cats. This is because the official judging standard does not specify an ideal weight range, whereas this is specified for dog breeds. Size can be a guide, but this is not a reliable indicator. For example, breeds such as the British and American shorthairs may have a similar height to Oriental breeds like the Siamese, but they have a much heavier, thick-set appearance, usually described as 'cobby'. In addition, while queens and toms in smaller breeds weigh about the same, in the case of larger cats such as the Maine Coon, toms are likely to be bigger and heavier.

Why is Feline Obesity Increasing?

One reason for the increase in feline obesity is that cats are living significantly longer than in the past, thanks to advances in veterinary care. If cats carry on eating the same amount of food but take progressively less exercise as they grow older, they will almost inevitably gain weight.

Weight gain is made even more likely because more cats are neutered nowadays. Neutering is essential in the case of tom cats living in the home, to prevent them from spraying urine as a territorial marker. In the case of queens, the potentially large numbers of kittens that they can produce means that it is important to control their fertility. Neutering also serves to protect against serious disorders of the reproductive tract, such as pyometra. It also eliminates the persistent, loud calls made by queens seeking a mate, often through the night, which can lead to complaints from neighbours.

The hormonal changes that result from this surgery, known as castration in the case of toms and spaying in the case of queens, mean that neutered cats need less food. They also become less active, again reducing the quantity of food required. Neutered toms do not wander as far from home, maintaining much smaller territories

and being less inclined to fight, while spayed queens do not have the demands of pregnancy.

Cats living in urban areas actually have smaller territories than those living in rural environments, and they have to share these areas with other cats in the neighbourhood. They therefore tend not to roam as much as their wild relatives, whose size of territory is determined by the availability of prey. In areas where prey is scarce, the population density of wild cats is lower and cats wander more widely, which means they use more energy.

Many domestic cats get little exercise as they often stay close to home rather than roaming as they would in the wild.

In some areas, it is simply not safe to allow cats to venture out because of the dangers of traffic. Furthermore, fears over the theft of pure-bred cats means that some owners are reluctant to allow their pets out to wander on their own, and so they are kept permanently in the home. Living indoors in warmth and comfort means that the energy requirements of such cats are significantly less than those of free-roaming cats, leaving them vulnerable to obesity. Add neutering and growing older to the mix, and the likelihood of such cats putting on weight is dramatically increased.

The Sphynx is a breed that typifies the problems of cats that live indoors and are prone to obesity. It is sometimes called the hairless cat because it retains very little fur on its body, although there are likely to be wisps evident on the extremities, such as the tips of the ears and the tail. Outside, deprived of the natural insulation provided by fur, the Sphynx could easily become chilled, and therefore would use up energy trying to maintain its body temperature. Indoors, however, it lives at an equitable temperature with no risk of becoming cold, and with relatively less energy expenditure. It's food requirements are therefore considerably reduced.

Since all the domestic cat's basic needs with regard to food, warmth and shelter are met inside the house, it is not surprising that its level of activity is drastically lower than that of a stray out hunting for its own food. Cats are intelligent predators by nature, so an indoor cat can easily become bored, especially if left on its own for much of the day. This can result in the cat eating more than necessary, particularly if it is left a plentiful supply of food. See chapter 5 for ideas for encouraging these cats to become more active.

The Food Issue

In the wild, cats naturally eat a high-protein, low-carbohydrate diet and expend lots of energy when hunting for food. The development of manufactured food for cats, however, removed the need for hunting and introduced new ingredients into the cat's diets. The way we now feed our cats is undoubtedly contributing to the increasing incidences of obesity.

Prepared cat food originally came in the form of frozen or canned food. With frozen food, you had to thaw out and cook the required quantity for your pet each day. Canned food offered a more balanced feeding option, being supplemented with vitamins, minerals and other ingredients, and the quantity of food offered to the cat at a single meal would be dependent on, and limited by, the size of the can.

With both frozen and canned food, there was little point in overfeeding your cat because any leftovers would soon dry up and be ignored by your pet. You cannot simply pile up your pet's food bowl with these types of foods. Cats are fastidious in their feeding habits, and tend not to eat food that has started to lose its moisture content, drying up and deteriorating in quality. Furthermore, you would soon notice the leftover food beginning to smell and possibly attracting flies, especially during warmer weather. Conversely, overfeeding is very easy if you are using dry cat food for your pet.

LOOKING AFTER YOUR CAT'S TEETH

Whatever type of food you use, it is a good idea to brush your cat's teeth if you can. If you have a kitten, it will be possible with patience to train your pet to allow you to brush its teeth. Use a toothbrush and toothpaste specially designed for this purpose. Never use ordinary toothpaste, because this is likely to be harmful. If you have an older cat that has an accumulation of tartar on its teeth, ask your vet to remove it. The earlier this is done, the easier and less traumatic it will be for your pet.

Dry Food

The advent of dry cat food has significantly altered the way in which we feed our cats. There is no doubt that the availability of dry food has made it easier to keep cats in the home, but it is also a key reason for the current epidemic of obesity affecting the domestic cat population. This is not an inherent fault of the food itself, but rather the way in which it is used by cat owners.

The Drawbacks

Originally, people were concerned about using dry cat food owing to possible links with the medical condition feline urological syndrome (FUS). This condition results in blockages in a cat's urinary tract caused by a build-up of small stones. These pass out of the bladder and get washed down into the urethra, which carries urine out of the body, forming a blockage. The effects of FUS are potentially life-threatening, so it requires emergency treatment. Initially, an affected cat is restless, and instead of squatting down to urinate as normal, will tend to crouch, producing little if any urine. This accumulates in the bladder, which is then at risk of rupturing unless the obstruction is relieved.

One of the contributory factors in the formation of blockages of this type can be a relatively high level of magnesium in the diet. Manufacturers of dry foods have now reduced the level of this mineral in their food. They have also lowered the pH level in the food, because stones are less likely to form when the urine is acidic than when it is alkaline. This is one of the reasons why cats cannot be fed dog food, because it is not formulated to lower the pH level of their urine.

A related problem is that cats fed on dry foods tend not to drink as much as they need in order to

compensate for the lack of fluid in their diet. Dry food typically contains just 10 per cent water, compared with wet food that may consist of about 75 per cent; the greater moisture content approximates much more closely to a cat's natural food. The lack of fluid in dry food means that a cat's urine is more likely to become concentrated. As a result, the risk is greater that mineral salts will crystallize and form a blockage.

In the early days of dry foods, cats seemed less inclined to feed on such diets, especially if they had been accustomed to canned or fresh food. Today, however, the palatability issue has been overcome, but the question remains as to whether dry foods are actually better than wet food.

The Benefits

One area where dry foods are beneficial is in terms of dental health. Cats do not tend to suffer from cavities, but are likely to develop a build-up of tartar if fed on wet food. This begins as plaque, which is a combination of tiny food particles and bacteria, and over time becomes impregnated with mineral salts and hardens into tartar. It creates a greyish-yellow appearance at the base of the teeth, ultimately spreading down to the gums where it causes severe inflammation.

Deposits of tartar need to be removed to prevent them from eroding the gum and weakening the teeth in their sockets. If this occurs, bacteria can penetrate to the root of the teeth and cause an abscess. There is a risk of bacteria spreading around the body, triggering a more widespread and serious infection. Using dry food helps to prevent an accumulation of tartar because it is more abrasive than wet food, helping to wipe away sticky deposits on the teeth. This is important because cats are living longer than ever, and need to keep their teeth in good condition.

If you have a long-haired cat, deposits of wet food may be left on the hair around the jaws after each meal; these are likely to dry and cause an unpleasant odour. In some cases, hairs can become stuck in deposits of tartar around the teeth, so pay particular attention when grooming the mouth area of your pet. You may need to clip back the fur in this area, although using a dry diet does mean that this should be less of a problem.

Overall, however, the main reason that dry diets are now so popular with cat owners is simply that they are convenient. They represent a much more concentrated source of energy than wet food, with only relatively small amounts being required.

Fresh Food

Providing your cat with a balanced diet based on fresh food is difficult. The best way of doing this would be to purchase frozen rodents (such as those available for snakes) and defrost them for your cat. These represent the cat's natural food, providing a balance that is missing if selective cuts of meat are used instead. In the days before prepared foods were widely available, vets used to see nutritional problems linked with fresh food diets in which one particular cut of meat was used as the main basis of a cat's diet. Too much prime steak, for example, causes skeletal problems because it contains virtually no calcium. Offal can also be harmful. One of the most common dietary problems seen in cats used to be hypervitaminosis A, resulting from an intake of too much vitamin A,

Cats need to take in more fluid if they are fed only dry food. Fresh food, such as these fish being caught by feral cats, is naturally high in moisture.

contained in a diet of liver. This has harmful effects on the cat's skeleton, triggering the development of bony spurs on the vertebrae in the head and neck region, causing pain and lameness.

Even a diet based largely around fish has its drawbacks. Dependence on oily fish such as mackerel may be implicated in the condition known as steatitis, also called yellow fat disease because of its characteristic signs in the body. More serious symptoms, including fever, loss of appetite and changes in the white blood cell count, are also likely to arise with this condition.

Although it is possible to devise suitable diets based on fresh food and supplements to keep cats in good health, this requires careful planning and shopping. In comparison, modern formulated foods have made it much easier to keep cats in good health, and nutritional deficiencies are essentially unheard of, provided that the food is properly stored and used before its recommended date on the packaging.

Assessing Your Pet

Cats that regularly go out and roam are less likely to become overweight than those that live inside the home on a permanent basis. This does not mean that all cats that are kept indoors will become overweight, but their cosseted lifestyle does put them at greater risk of weight gain. The situation is not helped by the difficulty of working out the ideal weight for a cat. Ideal weights for cats can vary greatly, particularly in the case of larger breeds. Typical weights for most cats are likely to fall between 2.7 and 5.4 kg (6 and 12 lb), but in the case of the largest breeds such as the Maine Coon, a mature tom may easily weigh nearly double this upper figure without being overweight. This is why assessing your cat's body condition is so important in judging whether the cat is at its ideal weight or not (see pages 24–6).

The more active a cat is, the less likely it is to gain weight. For playful young cats, obesity is seldom an issue.

Weighing Your Cat

In order to keep your cat fit and ensure that it does not pile on unwanted pounds, you need to weigh the cat regularly. This will alert you to any gain in weight before it becomes serious, enabling you to take appropriate action at an early stage when it is much easier to correct the problem. If you are measuring your cat's weight in pounds, you need to have scales that measure in both pounds and ounces to keep a check on small increases. Otherwise, you may suddenly find that your pet has gained 1 lb (0.45 kg). Although this may not sound much, it actually represents a

It is important to monitor your cat's weight regularly and accurately. Weigh your cat before feeding.

16 per cent gain in weight for a cat that should weigh around 6 lb (2.7 kg) – a significant figure. Being able to monitor your cat's weight loss in ounces or grams will also help you to keep an effective check on your pet's progress.

Get a diary and use it to keep track of your cat's weight. Try to weigh your cat at roughly the same time each morning, before feeding. This will give you a standard baseline for comparative purposes.

Cats rarely co-operate sufficiently to sit on a pair of scales, so place your cat in a travelling basket first if necessary. Place the basket on the scales or carefully attach it to a spring balance, checking first that the base of the box is secure. Weigh the container separately and deduct this from the first figure in order to get the weight of your cat. If your cat is not overweight, weighing your pet twice a month should be adequate.

Changing Needs

Kittens will obviously put on weight as they mature, growing for at least six months or even longer in the case of bigger breeds that are slow to mature, such as colourpoint longhairs (also known as Himalayans). In order to meet a kitten's requirements, it is a good idea to use one of the special foods formulated for kittens that are now widely available. These provide a much more concentrated source of energy compared with routine maintenance diets (see pages 53–5). It is equally important not to continue using kitten food for an adult cat, because this is likely to provide too many calories.

As a guide, a kitten under four months of age is likely to require double the number of calories – around 125 calories per pound of body weight – than an older individual aged between six and nine months, whose growth is complete. Unless

you cut back on calorie intake, it is obvious that extra calories that are no longer required for growth will simply end up contributing to weight gain. Furthermore, in the case of adult cats, larger

While growing, kittens need more calories and more frequent meals than adult cats.

breeds weighing over 10 lb (4.5 kg) need fewer calories proportionally than small breeds, typically 5 to 10 calories less per pound of body weight.

Obesity is unlikely to be a problem in kittens, partly because they are growing fast, but also because they are very active. A kitten will also seek attention from you, so you are more likely to play with it, again helping to prevent excessive weight gain. Weight gain can start to occur from around the age of six months because cats are usually neutered at this time. This will be later in the case of those larger breeds, such as Persians, that may not become sexually mature until they are over a year old.

Training and Fitness

With a young cat, it is important to strike up a close bond with your pet, and to teach it to recognize its name. Although many people believe that cats cannot be trained like dogs, this is untrue. Cats are creatures of habit, and if you can train your cat to come to you when you call its name, you will increase future opportunities for exercise and good health.

Patterns of behaviour learned as a young cat are likely to remain with your pet as it grows older, and can be reinforced by regular repetition throughout its life. However, there is no need to reward your cat with a treat if it comes to you when called.

Developing a close bond with your pet will facilitate training and allow you to establish patterns of good behaviour.

If you do offer a treat, your cat will soon expect one on every occasion, and may start to pester you if you do not provide the required tidbit. React instead by praising your pet briefly, and making a fuss of your cat at the same time. You could do so by playing a game with your pet, or encouraging it to play with a toy. This type of activity is a more beneficial treat than food.

Feeding Etiquette

It is important to develop a routine at mealtimes. Kittens are likely to need feeding four times a day in the immediate post-weaning period, with the feeding frequency reducing to two meals a day by the time they are about a year old. Although it is natural behaviour for a cat to eat small amounts frequently, going back and forth to the food bowl as many as 20 times a day, this can make it hard for you to monitor your pet's food intake. Try to persuade your cat to eat each meal in one go. You will know from the manufacturer's feeding guidelines just how much food is required, and you should not offer more than your pet will consume at a single sitting.

You should also avoid offering table scraps, especially at the time that you are eating or immediately afterwards. Otherwise, you are likely to find that your cat plagues you for offerings on every occasion. If you give in, the cumulative effect will soon be evident as your cat starts to gain weight. Equally, do not top up your cat's food bowl with any leftovers later, because this will have the same effect. Human foods are not always suitable for cats in any case. Foods such as bacon rinds can be particularly dangerous because of their high salt content, especially in the case of older cats who may already be suffering from kidney or heart failure and require a low-sodium diet. This also applies to other prepared meats, such as ham. Fish is especially dangerous because of the many bones that can be in it, which could stick in your cat's throat, while chicken can also be hazardous because of small bones. Cats are not likely to find the offer of vegetables appealing.

Do not be misled into thinking that cat treats are free from calories. Used occasionally, these are unlikely to have any serious impact on your pet's weight, but if you offer them on a daily basis, the likelihood is that your pet will gain weight. There is no need to give treats for any reason. If your cat is receiving a balanced diet, an excess of components such as fat-soluble vitamins could actually prove to be harmful. In addition, if you give your cat treats regularly, you are likely to find that your pet pesters you determinedly if you withdraw them. It is better to use them only occasionally. Used carefully, treats can help you to train your cat, such as persuading your pet to come inside after being put out last thing at night. However, if you offer treats for this reason on a daily basis, all you may do is encourage the cat to sit outside waiting for the treat.

WARNING SIGNS OF HAIRBALLS

If your cat has developed the habit of wandering back and forth to its food bowl rather than eating its food in one sitting, this will not only make it more difficult for you to monitor your pet's food intake, but could also mean that you miss one of the key signs of a hairball. When a cat grooms itself, it licks its coat, and some of the hairs will stick to the rough surface of the tongue, particularly during a moult. These can easily be swallowed, accumulate in the stomach and cause a partial blockage.

An affected cat will not be able to eat as much food as usual because of the obstruction, and will tend to pick constantly at its food. If a cat usually eats its food readily in one sitting, a change in this habit could indicate a hairball, but if your cat is always a picky eater, you may not notice that there is a problem. It is important to be aware of this situation, so that appropriate treatment, usually consisting of a laxative, can be given to ensure that the hairball passes out of the stomach and through the intestinal tract.

Regular daily brushing of long-haired cats will help to minimize the risk of hairballs, and is especially important in the moulting season. Brushing helps to remove much of the shed hair from the coat, so it will not end up being swallowed by the cat when it grooms itself. Studies have revealed that Persians may spend up to 30 hours every week grooming themselves, but you can help these breeds by brushing them.

If your cat wanders outdoors, it may eat grass. This acts as an emetic, making the cat sick, hopefully vomiting up the hairball in the process. There are now special foods formulated to lessen the likelihood of your cat suffering from this problem (see page 55). Keep an eye on this, otherwise your cat may lose weight and become malnourished due to the effects of the hairball in its stomach.

Lifestyle Considerations

Cats are not by nature very active animals. Their lives consist of periods of intense activity, when they are hunting, followed by rest. Domestic cats are even less active than their wild relatives, because they do not need to hunt for prey. Another aspect of their behaviour that contributes to an impression of lethargy is the fact that they tend to be crepuscular in their habits, becoming more active at dusk rather than during the daytime.

Cats sleep on average for twice as long as most mammals, and they are likely to spend up to 16 hours asleep every day. This depends partly on their age, with young and elderly cats sleeping for longer than adults, but it can also be a reflection of their lifestyle – cats that are left alone will sleep for longer than those that have company during the day. This can be an advantage if you are out for much of the day, but you must then spend time playing with your cat to keep your pet active when you come

Cats often spend up to 16 hours a day sleeping and tend to become more active at dusk.

WHY IS MY CAT OVERWEIGHT?

If your cat is overweight, you need to analyze the dietary and lifestyle factors that could have caused the problem in the first place. Once you have pinpointed the causes, you will be able to target your pet's weight-loss programme to tackle these causes most effectively, thereby helping to ensure long-term weight loss. Ask yourself the following questions, then if you say 'yes' to one of them, turn to the relevant chapter to see how best to take appropriate action.

1 Am I providing my cat with too much food? (see chapter 4)

2 Have I had my pet neutered and not adjusted its diet? (see chapter 6)

3 Could my cat be obtaining food elsewhere? (see chapter 4)

4 Is my pet becoming older and less active? (see chapter 6)

5 Am I giving my cat too many treats and tidbits? (see chapter 4)

6 Are other members of the family feeding the cat as well? (see chapter 4)

home. If you do not, the cat is more likely to become overweight through lack of exercise.

Many people are reluctant to allow their cats out to roam when they are away from home themselves. Some fear that their cat may be stolen, particularly pure-bred cats, while others worry that their cat could be injured or killed by traffic. Road accidents are a very real danger, but permitting your cat to go outside into the garden if you have one will give your pet the opportunity to take exercise in an area that is reasonably safe.

In addition to vehicles, there may be other dangers on the street at night in the guise of predators such as urban foxes. Although cats can generally escape from foxes, leaping up trees, or onto walls or buildings away from danger, cats that are seriously overweight are likely to face much greater difficulty eluding this type of threat. Try limiting your pet to short periods outside rather than allowing it to roam all night; training your pet to return when called by name should help you to prevent your cat from straying too far from home. A cat's urge to roam at night will be more of a problem on warm summer evenings than when the weather is very cold or wet.

Cat Flaps

If you decide that you want your cat to be able to come and go when you are not at home, thereby allowing it to exercise on its own during the day, you will need to fit a cat flap. There are various designs on the market, with the simplest operating on a swing basis. The cat can push its way in and out as it wants if the flap is hinged in both directions; flaps that are hinged in one direction only are also available and these can be useful if you are in the process of toilet training your cat.

It is usually not too difficult to train a cat to use a cat flap. Place your cat on the inside, then go outside yourself, partially lift the flap and call the cat through to you. Once your pet has come through the flap, go inside and encourage the cat to join you again on the inside. Before long, your cat will be pushing through the flap without any hesitation.

The major drawback of this design is that it allows other cats from the

A cat flap allows your pet to come and go freely – various types and mechanisms are available.

neighbourhood to enter your home as well as your own pet. These visitors may steal your cat's food and possibly soil your house – and you could well blame your own pet unfairly.

A better option may be to install a cat flap that operates on a magnetic basis. This entails fitting your pet with an elasticated collar to which a magnet is attached. As the cat approaches the cat flap, the magnet opens the flap so that only your pet can gain access to your home. Unfortunately, cats often lose their collars when they are out. Losing a collar with a magnet would, of course, mean that the cat cannot get back inside the home until you return. It is always worth searching for the lost collar and magnet in the areas your cat frequents. Most magnetic cat flaps are supplied with several spare magnets, but check before you buy from the pet store or manufacturer.

There is a likelihood, of course, that your cat could be going elsewhere to obtain food, perhaps being fed by a neighbour, which may explain why your pet is overweight. The only way to guarantee that this is not happening is to accompany your pet outdoors or confine it indoors.

THE DANGERS OF NIGHT VISION

Cats are probably at greater risk of being harmed on the roads at night when there is less traffic than during busier daylight hours. Ironically, this is because they can see better in the dark than we can. Cats have a mirror-like arrangement at the back of each eye. Light passes through the eye and hits the retina, where the image forms. Cats have more rod cells here than humans, which gives them much better night-time vision. Behind the retina there is a reflective layer known as the *tapetum lucidum* that directs light back through the retina, improving the image.

Unfortunately, a bright light shone into a cat's eyes after dark is likely to dazzle the cat. This happens when a cat is caught in a vehicle's headlights. The cat's eyes will shine in the darkness at this stage, as a result of the reflective layer, and the dazzled cat will have less time to react to the oncoming danger. A cat that is not overweight will fare better than an obese individual because it will be able to move out of the way of danger more quickly.

Although your cat may prefer to roam at night, it is therefore much safer to keep your pet indoors, encouraging your cat to spend longer outside during the day. Key ingredients in the cat's diet, such as taurine, are vital for its vision.

Feline Networking

In most areas today, and certainly in urban areas, cats live at much greater densities than would normally be the case in the wild. They will interact with each other under these circumstances, developing a complex network of behaviour patterns aimed at avoiding conflict. There will be a series of what to us are invisible paths crossing gardens, and cats have set areas where they can rest during the day, without being challenged by other cats in the neighbourhood. These movements help to provide them with more exercise than would be the case if they were confined indoors. It also provides them with greater mental stimulation.

Two kittens growing up together in the same home are likely to remain close throughout their lives, sleeping and playing together both indoors and outside, but neighbouring cats rarely form close bonds with each other. Although allowing your cat outdoors should help to ensure that your pet remains fit and is at less risk of becoming overweight, you will need to ensure that your cat's vaccinations are kept up-to-date, with booster jabs as required. Where cats are living in relatively high numbers and crossing the same areas, such as climbing through gaps in a fence, infections can easily spread.

Fighting can occur among cats outdoors, especially between unneutered toms but also between other individuals that come into conflict. Cats rarely inflict serious wounds on each other during a fight. What tends to happen is that the weaker individual runs off, pursued over a short distance by the rival cat. However, apart from the risk of injury, fighting can carry other health risks. The viral illness known as feline leukaemia, for example, is transmitted from the saliva of an infected individual as the result of a bite. Neutering your cat is a good way to lower the risk of fights, most of which occur between unneutered toms. This does, of course, mean that you will need to be vigilant about weight gain.

Some cats are quite bold about seeking food in other people's homes, which can be a particular drawback of having a cat flap. For this reason, it is always better to choose a design that operates on the basis of a magnet on the cat's collar, because this will only allow the resident cat into the home. You may not be aware that your cat actually has another source of food, although it is always a possibility if your pet seems to be gaining weight, or not losing any, in spite of your best efforts, and is spending more time outdoors than in the past.

It is frequently not easy to track exactly where your cat is wandering, because your pet will find its way through gaps in the fence or hedge around your property, but you could try sticking a note with a phone number in a conspicuous position on your cat's collar. Make the tone light-hearted, so that anyone who is feeding your cat will be aware

Cats that live together often form close bonds, while neighbouring cats develop a complex network of behaviour.

of the problem that you are facing, although there is the possibility that your pet could be venturing into their home and stealing food in their absence.

If your cat is going in and out of the other home through a cat flap, this can be a difficult problem to resolve, and in some cases it may be that the person who is feeding your cat is deliberately doing so, in the mistaken belief that the cat is hungry, without appreciating that your pet is on a diet. You need to handle this situation with some diplomacy, and if you are lucky, you may even be able to persuade the other person to play with your cat rather than feed it, thereby helping your pet to lose weight rather than the other way around.

The other situation that may arise when you put your cat on a diet is that your pet instinctively reacts by spending longer trying to catch prey, although scavenging will always remain the preferred option. This is perhaps the best outcome of all, certainly initially, because your pet is likely to be too slow to catch any birds or other creatures, but will be taking more exercise on a regular basis as a result. As your cat starts to become fitter, however, you will need to take action at that stage.

CONSULT A VET

It is a good idea to consult a veterinarian before finalizing your cat's diet, to ensure that no underlying medical condition is present, and also to obtain guidance on the best way forward for your particular pet. Since many veterinary practices now run clinics for overweight pets, it is beneficial to seek the help and encouragement of the staff there. This really can make a difference, especially because you will need to deny treats that your pet has enjoyed in the past, and this can be difficult.

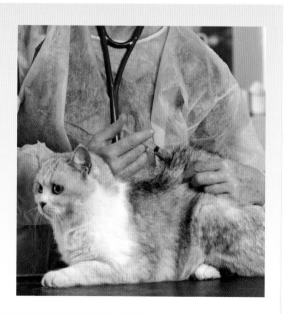

Dietary Considerations

Cats generally prefer to eat freshly cooked or 'wet' food that is traditionally sold in cans, because these are the closest in texture to their natural prey. Wet foods are now available in foil packs and plastic pouches as well as cans, with the basic ingredients being very similar. Whereas cans tend to offer food for a day or more, packs and pouches are usually designed to provide a single meal. This saves you from having to keep a large can of strong-smelling cat food in your refrigerator, although you could use a plastic cover to seal it once it has been opened.

Cats usually prefer their food to be warm and will be reluctant to eat food from the fridge until it has warmed up. Single-meal packs, however, can be stored at room temperature, which enhances the likelihood that your cat will eat them readily. Individual portions also mean that it should be possible to match the amount of food that you are offering to your cat's appetite. If you are using fresh food, it is especially important to encourage your cat to eat the entire meal at a single sitting so that the food does not deteriorate.

Semi-moist foods are also supplied in sachets, but are lighter than canned food, containing less water, typically around 35 per cent, which is half that of wet food. Although these foods may look appealing, they often contain sugar as a preservative, which is not part of a cat's natural diet. They are currently far less popular than dry food, but if you are using these products, read the labels carefully for hidden ingredients.

Dry food has a minimal water content, which helps to explain why it does not deteriorate as rapidly as wet food when tipped into a food bowl. It also represents a concentrated source of nutrition, so that cats only have to eat a small amount to meet their nutritional requirements.

Measuring Food

Before feeding your cat any type of packaged food, it is important to check the feeding instructions on the pack. The quantity of food that different cats need will vary, depending not just on the type of food that you are using, but also on the brand that you have chosen. It is very easy to start overfeeding your cat simply by not familiarizing yourself with the amount required, based on the manufacturer's recommendations.

Even if you are only changing your cat's food to another type within the same range, it is still important to check the quantity that is needed. Overfeeding your cat on a regular basis is the most common cause of obesity. This is especially likely in the case of dry food, partly because the quantity that your cat requires to meet its needs can appear so small that you instinctively feel obliged to top it up. This can be especially tempting if you have used wet food before, where a much larger amount is necessary.

Many owners fail to measure the amount of dry food accurately. Although a measuring container is not usually supplied with cat food, you can make one very easily, using a clean, empty plastic yoghurt pot or similar container. Weigh out the amount of food recommended for your pet carefully and tip this into the container. Shake the food down until it is level, then mark this point on the side of the pot. Alternatively, cut down the container with a pair of scissors to the appropriate height. In future, you can simply scoop up the requisite amount of dry food using the container without having to weigh it each time, before tipping the food directly into your cat's feeding bowl.

Always follow the manufacturer's recommendations on food quantities. Cats need less dry food as it is more concentrated than wet or semi-wet food.

FUSSY EATERS

There are many different flavours of cat food now available, but the basic ingredients of these foods should otherwise be the same, offering a complete, balanced diet. Cats can become rather fixated on flavours, with these preferences actually starting to develop in kittens while they are still in the womb. It is therefore a good idea to encourage kittens to take a range of foods when they are young to prevent them from becoming finicky about their food in later life.

Cats can sometimes be very fussy in their feeding habits, although the dramatic increase in levels of feline obesity over recent years would seem to belie this. Even changing between brands of wet food can be problematic, and if you leave your cat in a boarding cattery, you may need to tell them what type of food your pet is used to – it is not unknown for cats to refuse to eat when presented with unfamiliar food in a strange environment.

FOOD BOWLS

Unfortunately, the size of food bowls sold for cats in pet stores bears no relationship to the amount of food that a cat actually requires. Their design has not really changed much since the days when people fed their cats on fresh and canned food, whereas only a much smaller quantity is needed if you are feeding your pet a diet of dry food, because it is a much more concentrated source of nutrition. In short, food bowls are too big for the amount of food required.

It is therefore impossible to judge the correct amount of food to serve your cat just by tipping out the food directly into the bowl. You need to measure it accurately, in accordance with the instructions on the pack. There may be a measuring scoop included in some packs of cat food, but you could easily make one from an old, clean yoghurt pot or similar plastic container (see page 46). Either pour the required amount of food for your cat into the container, or use the container to scoop the food out of the packet. If you have not done this before, you may be surprised at the small amount of food that is actually required – and just how big the food bowl is in comparison.

Overfeeding

There used to be a belief that cats were not as greedy as dogs, and so could be trusted not to overeat when provided with more food in their bowl than was strictly necessary. Unfortunately, this is not true when they have free access to dry food, and regular overfeeding in this way will encourage over-consumption and weight gain. The cat's natural instincts to obtain food remain so strong that it will take advantage of a surplus, even if this is available on a constant basis.

The worst thing that you can do, therefore, is to fill up your cat's bowl and wait for your pet to empty it, then refill it, as this will happen much more quickly than it should. If you measure the food carefully, however, you can put the correct daily quantity into the bowl each morning and allow your cat to eat this throughout the day. In fact, this allows your pet to display more natural feeding behaviour, with cats tending to nibble at their food, eating as many as 20 small meals over the course of a day. It is more difficult to adopt this approach with wet food, as it is unpleasant to have this sitting around for any length of time.

In addition, free-feeding of this type is not recommended if you have a dog in your home, because the dog will attempt to steal the cat's food as well as eating its own. Under these circumstances, it is better to train your cat to eat its food in one sitting, but divide it up into portions during the course of a day. Adult cats can simply be fed morning and evening, allowing you to match your cat's food intake to its appetite and overcoming this problem.

Another reason that some people make the mistake of overfilling their cat's bowl with food is because they are worried that their cat will be hungry while they are out at work, especially if they are delayed on their journey home. Your cat will not come to harm under these circumstances. In fact, wild cats often go for a day or more without eating anything at all if they have not been able to make a kill, and it is actually as a result of this instinct that cats overeat when presented with an excess of food.

If you remain concerned, however, you can invest in a timed feeding tray. These are very easy to operate, running off a battery. You simply place the food in the tray before you go out, set the timer and place the unit where your cat normally eats. The lid lifts up at the pre-set time, allowing your pet access to the food inside. Some units of this type incorporate two separate feeders, allowing your cat to be given two separate meals in your absence.

HOW MANY CALORIES?

The average daily calorie requirement for a free-roaming cat has been estimated at 70 kcal per kg of body weight for a fully grown cat and 200 kcal per kg for a kitten. This will vary depending on factors such as how much exercise the cat is getting, its age and also the climate in which it lives. The following list gives the typical calorie content of various types of commonly sold cat food aimed at adult cats.

- Wet food   175 kcal per 100 g
- Semi-moist food   300 kcal per 100 g
- Dry food   470 kcal per 100 g

Breed-Specific Feeding

Ordinary cat food should be more than adequate for all cats, but there are now some breed-specific diets available for the most popular breeds. For example, the compact shape of the Persian longhair's face makes it difficult for it to feed. While most cats spend less than an hour eating every day, Persians need to spend longer feeding. Studies have revealed that these cats eat in a different manner from other breeds when given dry food. Persians feed by picking up pieces of dry food using the underside of the tongue, after which they fold the tongue over into the mouth, hopefully flicking the pieces of food inside. They often appear to be eating a lot, but in reality much of the food is dropped back into the food bowl. A breed-specific dry food is now available for Persians, with almond-shaped pieces that are easier for them to pick up.

Persians spend longer feeding than other breeds, as their physionomy makes picking up food difficult.

Cornish and Devon Rexes, with their sparse fur, require more calories daily to help keep them warm.

each breed's coat. The typical fur structure of most cats is comprised of three layers: an outer layer of long guard hairs; a middle layer of shorter, secondary guard hairs, known as awn hairs; and a layer of down hairs lying closest to the body, which are the shortest hairs and have a wool-like texture. The down hairs trap warm air next to the skin, helping to insulate the cat's body.

The mutations underlying the distinctive appearance of the two Rex breeds have altered this basic arrangement. In the case of the Cornish Rex, the outer guard hairs have largely disappeared, and the awn hairs are much shorter than normal, so they are barely longer than down hairs. The coat is about half as thick as that of a normal cat, with the diameter of the individual hairs being reduced as well. This creates the distinctive waves in the Cornish Rex coat, and leaves the cat more vulnerable to the cold. This breed naturally has a slightly higher body temperature than other cats, whose temperature is approximately 38.6°C (101.5°F), presumably to offset the increased heat loss from its body. In turn, this increases the Cornish Rex's daily calorie requirement by approximately 7 kcal per kg of body weight.

Diets aimed at long-coated cats contain specific adjustments to the fibre content in order to minimize the risk of hairballs. Special diets are also available for Maine Coon and Siamese cats, containing a range of key ingredients to help maintain them in good health, reinforcing their immune system.

There can also be slight differences in the quantity of food a cat requires based on its breed type. This is usually related to the structure of

The situation is more marked in the case of the Devon Rex, a breed that first appeared in 1960, approximately a decade after its Cornish counter-part. In this case, both the outer guard hair and the awn are virtually absent from the coat, which is therefore comprised mainly of down. Without the presence of guard hairs, the Devon Rex has a very sparse coat, and in some cases these cats may display bald patches on their bodies. Devon Rexes will readily roam outdoors, even in cold weather, but just like their Cornish counterpart, these cats do require additional food in order to stay warm.

A more extreme example is the rare Sphynx, or hairless cat. The breed does, in fact, have a very fine covering of hair on its body, often described by breeders as 'peach fuzz', because of its similarity to the skin of a peach, as well as longer hair on the extremities of its body, notably on the ears and tail. While the breed is susceptible to the cold, it is also at risk outdoors in hot weather because of the danger of sunburn, which in some cases can lead to skin cancer. As a result, the Sphynx is kept almost exclusively indoors rather than being allowed to wander outside, where it would be vulnerable to attacks by other cats because of the exposure of the skin over its entire body. As with the Rexes, the Sphynx may have a larger appetite than other cats because of its lack of fur. One advantage of this lack of fur, however, is that it may be easier to see if a Sphynx is becoming overweight.

The Sphynx has a very distinctive appearance, thanks to its lack of fur. This, in turn, affects its nutritional needs and care.

Certain breeds may be at particular risk of obesity, due to factors ranging from coat type to lifestyle. If you have one of these breeds, it is particularly important that you monitor your pet's weight regularly and take action before a problem develops:

- Cornish Rex
- Devon Rex
- Persian Longhair
- Ragdoll
- Siamese
- Sphynx

Lifestage Diets

Specially formulated lifestage diets may represent a significant breakthrough in the battle against obesity in cats. They were developed on the basis that a cat's nutritional requirements vary with age. A diet for kittens, for example, typically has a fat content of 10–30 per cent, whereas 6–9 per cent fat is adequate for older cats that are neutered and living indoors.

A manufacturer's range may include a diet for young kittens up to four months old; an older kitten food that should be used until the young cat is one year old; an adult diet for cats up to the age of 10; and a food specially formulated for older cats. There may even be a food catering for the needs of elderly cats from 15 years onwards, but the options offered by different brands do vary, so you will need to check which is the best one for your particular cat.

The reason that the quantities recommended on the pack vary within each category is a reflection of the fact that different breeds vary in size, which influences their energy requirements and therefore the quantity of food they should be fed. Large breeds generally require more energy than smaller ones, although not on a directly proportional basis. Bigger cats need slightly fewer calories on a per kg/lb of body weight basis. This is because of the relationship between body weight and surface area, the latter influencing the rate of heat loss from the body and therefore the energy input required by the cat to keep its body temperature constant. A cat with a body weight of 4.5 kg (10 lb) has a surface area of 0.26 sq m (0.31 sq yds), but an individual that is double this weight does not have double the surface area. Its surface area is just 0.41 sq m (0.49 sq yds), so it does not need to expend as much energy on maintaining its core body temperature.

A cat that is living permanently in the home also requires fewer calories, because the temperature within the home is higher than outside and so the cat uses less energy to stay warm. This is also true of cats that have been neutered because they tend to be less active. You therefore need to monitor your cat's weight even if you are following the feeding instructions carefully, because these factors mean that your pet could have slightly different food requirements.

If you have a queen that becomes pregnant, her food requirements will soar by at least a quarter, especially towards the end of the pregnancy. She may need up to three times as much food while she is suckling her kittens, and will also drink much more during this period.

SPECIALIST DIETS

Kitten
Specially designed to meet the needs of young, growing cats, these diets have a significantly higher calorie content than adult food.

Post-neutering
A diet that helps to ensure that your cat's weight will not balloon after neutering, as will almost inevitably happen unless you change the amount of regular food that you offer to your pet.

Adult
Intended for adult cats that can wander freely, this may also include an anti-hairball component, as do a number of other diets on the market.

Senior
Foods that are specially formulated to delay the onset of the ageing process, being beneficial from seven years of age upwards, based on the latest research. They contain a carefully formulated mix of key ingredients to combat ageing, such as antioxidants, essential fatty acids and probiotics, combined with a reduction in calories. They are also likely to include an anti-hairball component.

Breed specific
Diets designed to cater for the particular feeding needs of popular breeds such as Persians and Maine Coons.

Indoor
Foods that reflect the decreased level of activity of most house cats that live permanently indoors, helping to guard against obesity and reduce litter-tray odour.

Hypoallergenic
Diets specially formulated to take account of possible food intolerances and allergies. These may also be useful for fussy eaters.

Lite
A low-calorie diet intended to prevent cats from becoming overweight and, more commonly, to aid cats in losing weight.

Feeding requirements vary depending on a cat's age, breed and activity level.

Feeding Preferences

There are a number of factors that influence the feeding preferences of cats. Their dietary preferences start to be formed before birth as a result of molecules that are passed across the placenta from the mother's body and those surrounding them in the amniotic fluid. This early conditioning is reinforced during the weaning process, with kittens being attracted to the food that their mother is eating. Subsequently, when introduced to a new food, cats may choose this alternative rather than their old food, but within a few days this preference starts to disappear.

Cats possess a much more acute sense of smell than humans and the main thing that draws a cat to its food is the odour. Manufacturers use special coatings on their food to enhance its attractiveness, with fats often used for this purpose on dry food, which is the least palatable option of the different types of cat food.

Once the cat has been drawn to the food bowl, the ease with which the food can be eaten becomes significant. In the case of dry food, the amount of strength that has to be applied to break the food is important.

The cat will also be influenced by the flavour of the food. Cats have a unique sense of taste, resulting from the presence of umami taste receptors. These can detect a compound called glutamate that is derived from an amino acid and related to sodium glutamate, which is a recognized flavour enhancer in human food. Cats do not recognize sweet tastes, presumably because they do not naturally consume carbohydrate, nor are their salt taste receptors effective. Cats rely heavily on acid taste receptors, and also use the bitter taste receptors at the back of the tongue to alert them to substances that could be poisonous. This defence is not foolproof, however. Many cats die each year from drinking ethylene glycol, which is a key ingredient of anti-freeze, and in spite of being deadly, cats seem oblivious to the danger.

A number of external considerations can also affect a cat's appetite. For example, cats often will not eat if their food bowl is placed in a busy area of the home, where there are likely to be people milling around. Cats prefer to eat in relatively quiet surroundings. Their food bowl should also not be placed next to their litter tray, which is likely to make them reluctant to eat.

If your cat is ill, do not be surprised if your pet loses interest in the brand of food that you usually serve. Illness often makes cats wary of returning to their former food in case this was the underlying cause of their illness. However, the phase will pass after about six weeks, when your cat will start eating its usual food again.

There is no significant evidence to show that just because prepared cat foods are carefully formulated to appeal to cats, this directly encourages them to overeat. As with wild cats,

Many factors can affect a cat's attitude to food, including odour, the location of its food bowl and, of course, taste.

when a domestic cat is hungry, its senses of smell and taste are heightened so that it can locate and then eat its food more easily. However, the senses that drew a cat to its food in the first instance become less acute as the cat consumes its meal. The key problem is that a cat may continue to eat persistently if allowed to do so, ingesting more calories than it requires to support its level of activity. These calories will then be converted by the body to unwanted fat. Some cats can be very fussy about their food, but this does not prevent them from becoming overweight.

One element that seems to be key in controlling a cat's appetite is a hormone called leptin. There is a chemical process, known as a biofeedback mechanism, within the cat's body that helps to regulate the cat's appetite. This is controlled by leptin, which is a chemical messenger produced by the body's fat cells, known as adipocytes.

It is important to keep feeding bowls clean and fresh, as cats can be fussy eaters. It will be harder to control what your cat is eating if it would rather search out food elsewhere than eat at home.

Leptin is carried in the blood to the part of the brain known as the hypothalamus. As the level of leptin rises, so this acts via the hypothalamus to curb the cat's appetite. Despite this, most domestic cats will eat whenever there is food available. If your pet refuses food, this is often a sign that your cat is ill, perhaps even suffering from toothache. Some cats find a dirty food bowl off-putting, which is why the bowl should be washed after each meal, as well as for hygienic reasons. A change of food, environment and sometimes a severe fright or the onset of thundery weather, may also cause a cat to lose its appetite, but only on a temporary basis.

Water and Milk

It is vital to remember that your pet must have free access to clean drinking water at all times, with cats that are being fed a diet of dry food requiring more water than those eating wet food. Water is essential to your pet's well-being, although it may not be possible to measure exactly how much your cat is drinking if your pet is allowed to wander freely outside, because cats often prefer to drink from garden ponds and other water sources.

The popular belief that cats need milk is just a myth. In fact, cats can suffer from an intolerance to milk more frequently than to any other item that is likely to feature in their diet. Siamese and similar breeds of eastern origin are especially likely to lack the enzyme known as lactase, which breaks down the milk sugar known as lactose. In the absence of this enzyme, lactose ferments in the intestinal tract, causing bloating and diarrhoea.

It is possible to buy special cat milk (from pet stores and supermarkets) that has been processed to remove the lactose, but milk is not a critical item in a cat's diet, and is certainly not necessary for a cat needing to lose weight. On the contrary, milk is high in fat and can be counterproductive when trying to slim down your pet. It should be the first thing to be dropped when a cat is on a diet, because all the nutrients that your cat needs will be present in the cat food you are providing. If you do offer milk to your cat, do not provide more than your pet will drink within a few minutes. You must also wash out the dish afterwards with detergent and then rinse it thoroughly.

Vegetarian Cats?

It is not possible to keep cats in good health on a vegetarian diet, because just like their wild relatives, domestic cats are obligate carnivores and it is therefore essential that they have meat in their diet. They can be fed fish, but this is not a natural food of the cat's ancestor, the African Wild Cat, and so should only be given in small amounts. Cats actually have quite a peculiar metabolism. For example, they need a higher level of protein in their diet than dogs, and the protein must be of animal rather than plant origin, because this contains key amino acids that are missing in vegetable protein.

The amino acid known as taurine is used in the production of bile salts, as well as being vital for the functioning of the retina in the eyes; a deficiency of taurine is likely to cause blindness. A shortage of taurine has also been linked with the condition known as dilated cardiomyopathy in cats. Arginine is another critical amino acid that needs to be present in a cat's diet, playing a key role in a vital metabolic cycle in the body.

Very serious symptoms have been noted in cats offered just a single meal from which this component of protein has been removed. Unsteadiness on the feet, increased production of saliva and lethargy occur rapidly should it be deficient.

In terms of fat metabolism, dogs can convert linoleic acid, an essential fatty acid, into arachidonic acid by a series of chemical reactions in their bodies, but cats cannot do this. Arachidonic acid is not present in plants to any significant extent, so this is another reason why cats cannot be kept in good health on a vegetarian diet. The same difficulty applies in the case of certain vitamins. Cats are not able to convert plant pigments known as carotenoids, which are found in carrots for example, to vitamin A, unlike most mammals. This vitamin

is essential for healthy eyesight and also gives some protection against infections. Cats are also unable to convert the amino acid tryptophan to the B vitamin known as niacin (nicotinic acid).

Zoologists believe that the specialized nutritional needs of cats are a reflection of their success as predators. In other words, because cats have evolved to be effective hunters, they have never had to resort to feeding on plant matter. As a consequence, it is impossible to meet all of a cat's nutritional requirements without including meat in its diet.

Changing Foods

When the time comes to switch your cat from a kitten diet to an adult one, it is important that you implement the change gradually over the course of several days. Do not make the change suddenly, because if your cat develops a digestive upset, this is likely to deter your pet from eating the new food for some time into the future. Gradually increase the percentage of new food, while cutting back on the kitten food. It is often a good idea to reduce the overall amount of food slightly for the first few days that your cat is eating the new food.

When your cat is fully grown, there is no reason why you should not feed it both dry and wet food, and this can actually have benefits. You can offer dry food in the morning, allowing your pet to pick at this throughout the day, and then offer a meal of wet food in the early evening. This is likely to be eaten readily, and you should then wash the food bowl thoroughly. A dirty food bowl can obviously make your pet ill, and it can also deter your cat from eating.

By offering your cat both types of food, you can switch to just one of these foods on a temporary basis if you need to for any reason. If your cat is used to only one type of food, it will be virtually impossible to wean it on to a new food quickly, especially from wet food to dry. If you have difficulty in persuading your cat to switch, try pouring some warm water over the dry food; ` do not saturate it, but just soften it slightly. This will give it a more attractive odour and texture for a cat that has previously been fed wet food.

If you are moistening dry food, never prepare more food than is required for a single meal. Dry food that has been treated in this way will deteriorate rapidly, and is likely to turn mouldy, so dispose of it if left uneaten after a couple of hours at room temperature. Once your cat has started to sample the moistened food, gradually reduce the amount of water that you add to the food over the course of several days, until your cat is eating it as it comes, straight from the packet.

When changing a cat's diet, for whatever reason, it is best to introduce new elements gradually.

Reducing Calories

Changing the type of food that you feed to your pet can help both to prevent and control weight gain in cats. There are a number of specialist diets available for this purpose (see page 55). As always when changing a cat's food, you need to carry out the change gradually over several weeks (see page 61). It is usually easier to switch between foods within a single manufacturer's range of products, because their basic formulations tend to be similar, providing a taste and texture with which the cat is already familiar, rather than switching to a totally new formulation.

Making dry food more palatable by pouring a little water over it has the added advantage of helping your pet feel full after each meal. As the water is absorbed, the food will swell up markedly in size and will occupy more space in your cat's stomach, although the actual calorie content will be no greater. Another advantage is that your cat will be taking in more liquid, although there is the disadvantage that any food not eaten after about 15 minutes will need to be discarded. While clearly you do not want to waste food, a cat that does not consume a whole meal within this timeframe will be consuming fewer calories.

As hunters, cats spend much of their time seeking food. If you are reducing the quantity of food that you are offering your pet, you may find that your cat appears to be hungry, following you and meowing to attract your attention for more food, especially at first. It can help at this stage to measure out the entire daily food allowance at the start of the day, and offer it to your cat in small portions, perhaps dividing it into six meals, whereas in the past you may have fed your cat just in the morning and evening. Your cat is therefore less likely to feel hungry, because eating more frequently will mean that there is food present in its stomach throughout the day. The action of eating will in itself make your cat less inclined to want more food. In addition, your pet is likely to become more active if you move the food bowl around, so that your cat needs to search for the food. Between meals, you could put a few pieces of your pet's daily ration of dry food inside a suitable toy. This may encourage your cat to play with the toy in order to obtain the extra food, promoting activity without increasing calories.

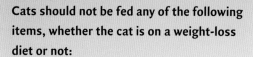

FOODS TO AVOID

Cats should not be fed any of the following items, whether the cat is on a weight-loss diet or not:
- Bacon, ham and other salty foods
- Very fatty foods, such as trimmings from meat
- Dairy products in some cases
- Onions and garlic
- Chocolate
- Alcohol

Stealing Another Cat's Food

This can be a real problem, often exacerbated by both pets being fed together and especially worsened when one pet is on a diet and is not getting as many calories as the other cat. The answer is to feed the cats individually, especially if you are relying on timed feeding trays. If you only have one area where it is suitable for your cats to eat, make sure that they are fed separately at different times.

Do not allow a situation to arise where an adult cat could steal a kitten's food. This is especially harmful to an overweight adult, because the kitten's food is much higher in calories than regular adult cat food. If the overweight cat eats the higher calorie food, this will worsen the problem for you when you are trying to slim down your older cat. Try to adjust feeding times to when you are around, so that you can supervise what is happening, especially if you are having difficulty in keeping your cats apart. African Wild Cats, from which the vast majority of domestic cats are descended, are solitary hunters, like the majority of wild cats. Even domestic cats that know each other well are unlikely to hunt collaboratively. Occasionally, however, one will watch the other stalking prey, and may sometimes pounce on the intended target if the bird or animal eludes its companion, but comes within its reach instead.

MEALTIMES

The rules for feeding are not hard and fast, however a dieting cat will benefit from a routine which you as the owner should try to stick to.

Kitten	3–4 times per day
Adult cat	2–3 times per day
Senior cat	3–4 times per day

HEALTHY TREATS

Putting your cat on a diet means that you will have to cut out the treats that your pet may previously have enjoyed on a regular basis. You may, however, be able to persuade your cat to take healthier options. Try small amounts of the following foods as trusted tidbits for your pet:

● Pilchards in tomato sauce
● Cooked white fish
● An occasional dental chew, which helps to keep the teeth clean
● Small pieces of chopped sweet apple

It is worth experimenting, within reason, to see if your cat can be induced to take small pieces of fruit or vegetables. Some cats will do so quite readily, while others will ignore such offerings. Some may happily nibble on small pieces of raw carrot or apple. You may also want to try a variety of vegetables that you cook for yourself, ranging from broccoli to green beans. There are some vegetables that, although they are perceived as being healthy for us, are seriously dangerous to cats. As a result, never allow your pet to eat any plant matter from members of the allium family. This includes onions and garlic, even if they are cooked, as well as chives.

Do not be tempted to use herbal supplements for your cat that are sold on

the basis of aiding weight loss in people. These may contain harmful ingredients as far as your cat is concerned, such as caffeine. The effects may vary, but they can include vomiting and diarrhoea, as well as hyperactivity, and an increase in heart rate, with the impact being potentially fatal.

Keep shopping out of reach of your pet, and be certain to keep the door to your refrigerator firmly closed at all times, to ensure that your cat cannot help itself to food when hungry.

Exercise

Dietary changes are only part of the solution in dealing with an overweight cat. In addition to reducing your pet's calorie intake, it is also important to increase your cat's level of activity. This will help to burn off more calories, as well as making your cat fitter and healthier overall. If you and your pet have a sedentary lifestyle, this is likely to be an underlying cause of the weight problem. Such a lifestyle is certainly not natural for a cat. Cats are athletes, and fitness is vital for their survival in the wild. They are supremely adapted to running, jumping, climbing and even swimming. This applies just as much to domestic cats as to their wild relatives, with all cats having a similar basic skeletal structure, with only minor variations reflecting shifts in their lifestyle – for example, how much they need to climb.

Athletic Abilities

The limbs of all cats are designed in such a way that they can run fast and adjust the position of their feet while doing so. This is extremely important because it helps a cat to change direction quickly when pursuing prey. Cats are described as being digitigrade, which means that they move on their digits (toes), rather than on the soles of their feet. This allows them to run quickly, building up their pace rapidly from a standing start – because they normally walk on their toes, they do not have to raise their front feet to start running.

Cats are also able to cover large areas of ground with each stride, thanks to their incredibly flexible backbone that bends rather like a spring, helping to propel them forwards. All cats have 30 bones in their vertebral column, except in the area of the tail. As the cat picks up speed, you can see its back curving as its legs tuck under the body, extending out again as the front legs are thrust forwards. This flexibility improves the cat's stride length, enabling it to extend its feet out in front of the body as it bounds along. This allows it to run quickly, and also to accelerate with great pace in order to close rapidly on its target, giving a greater element of surprise.

When cats decide to jump, their keen eyesight helps them to judge the distance involved accurately, so that they can land safely. The muscular strength for jumping is provided by the cat's powerful hind legs, which are also responsible for the main propulsive thrust when it is running. As it jumps, a cat tucks its front legs under its body, with the hind feet being the last part of the body to lift off and touch down, and it supports its weight on its front legs when it lands. The cat's tail acts as a counterbalance, rather like the pole carried by a tightrope walker in a circus, being extended horizontally behind the body at this stage.

Even if something goes wrong, the cat's quick reflexes allow it to swivel its body around so that it lands on its feet, minimizing the risk of serious injury, although the momentum of a fall from much over 6 m (20 ft) can mean its jaw hits the ground, resulting in a fracture.

The length of a cat's legs also assist it in jumping. Cats can leap considerable distances when necessary; pumas, for example, can leap almost 12m (40ft) at a single bound, which is over six times the length of their body. In the case of smaller cats, their jumping ability allows them to pounce on prey from some distance away, giving them the upper hand.

When cats swim, they use their legs and feet as paddles, with the hind legs providing propulsive power. The tail is extended horizontally behind the body, serving as a rudder to help the cat to steer. Air trapped in the coat may aid buoyancy, and also helps to prevent the body from becoming chilled. The cat can then simply shake its coat once it emerges on to land, removing much of the water, while the undercoat remains relatively dry. The cat's outer coat will dry off fairly quickly, and its insulating effect will prevent the cat from becoming too cold.

Cats are perfectly designed to run, jump and even
swim with supreme agility and grace. Weight gain
will hinder enjoyment of these activities.

CLAWS

Cats have claws that protrude from the end of the toes. These are normally drawn back out of sight and protected by sheaths unless the cat is about to attack, though it is not difficult to expose the claw by picking up the cat's foot. Claws are vital when the cat is climbing or fighting, and are important for grooming purposes as well. This is why surgery carried out to remove the claws of cats is cruel. Such surgery has a significant impact on a cat's natural behaviour patterns and may be a contributory factor in cases of obesity, restricting a cat's ability to climb, for example.

The condition of your cat's claws can be a good indicator of whether or not your pet is overweight. Under normal circumstances, a cat will wear down its claws by walking, climbing and scratching. This keeps the tips sharp and prevents them from becoming curled around. If you notice that your cat starts to become caught up by its claws around the home, on the cushion in its bed for example, this can indicate that your pet is not getting enough exercise.

The first thing you should do is arrange for your vet to trim back the tips of the claws, to make it easier for your pet to walk, and so take more exercise. You should also invest in

a scratching post for your pet, especially if your cat is living permanently indoors, although not all cats are inclined to use scratching posts (see pages 85–6 for a simple way to make one). If your pet finds catnip appealing (see pages 89–90), encourage your cat to use the scratching post by placing a catnip toy there, or even decorate the post with some catnip. The visual marks left by a cat's claws will indicate to another cat that the area is occupied. A cat will regularly return, not just to sharpen its claws but also to assert his command of the territory, so it can be a useful tool to lure a cat outside, especially following a spell of rain, when the scent will have washed off.

The Urge to Wander

Some cats have remarkable homing instincts, to the extent that they may journey many miles back to their former haunts after their owners have moved them to a new home. An analysis of 300 cases of this type revealed that cats travel 2–3 miles (3.2–4.8 km) per day on average, stopping off to hunt when they are hungry. This is much farther than most cats normally travel in the course of a day, although tom cats may wander quite widely in search of potential mates, frequently under cover of darkness.

Unspayed males sometimes disappear for days at a time, especially during the mating period,

Cats, especially males, have a natural urge to roam; our tendency to curb this by neutering and restricting them to the house can contribute to weight gain.

which typically extends from January through to September in the northern hemisphere and from October to June in the southern. They feed relatively little during this period, with the result that they return home out of condition, having lost a lot of weight.

Neutering, however, decreases a cat's instinct to wander, as well as encouraging weight gain due to hormonal changes. After surgery, neutered cats become less active and therefore require fewer calories, but they do not instinctively alter their feeding habits. It is therefore important that you make adjustments to your pet's diet, and equally that you encourage a neutered cat to remain active, because this will use up calories and help to prevent the cat from becoming overweight. Different breeds prefer different levels of activity, but all should be encouraged to take some exercise.

Cats naturally love to climb, and this aerobic exercise helps them to burn calories. Try not to discourage your cat from doing so.

Breeds and Needs

The behaviour of cats varies, with certain breeds being naturally more energetic and inclined to wander than others, which is largely a reflection of their ancestry. Whereas certain cats have been created primarily for show purposes, others have evolved naturally from working stock, and their instincts to spend time in an outdoor environment remain strong.

These include the Maine Coon, which is the oldest breed of cat from the New World. It was developed on the east coast of the United States in the state of Maine, from a variety of cats brought from Europe both by the early settlers and as ships' cats. Gradually, a recognizable type began to emerge, giving these cats a distinctive appearance, typically with tabby patterning, indicating their unrefined origins. The tabby stripes on the tail resemble a raccoon's tail markings, hence the second part of their name. The Maine Coon soon became inextricably linked with farmsteads, helping to control rodents.

The Norwegian Forest Cat has been shaped by very similar forces of natural selection as the Maine coon. It has also been suggested that this breed contributed to the development of the Maine Coon. Norwegian Forest Cats have existed in their homeland for centuries, again roaming on farms, but they did not become well known elsewhere until the 1930s. Unsurprisingly, they rank among the most active of breeds, possessing both a hardy nature and a weather-resistant coat.

At the other extreme, some breeds have acquired a particular reputation as being home-loving. This group includes the Persian Longhair. Bred in catteries for well over a century, these cats do not possess the keen outdoor instincts nor indeed display the same level of activity as the Maine Coon and the Norwegian Forest Cat. Persians have relatively short legs as well, which means that they are less able to run and jump and are therefore less inclined to engage in active exercise. Pampered in the home, Persians are at considerable risk of putting on weight.

The coats of most cats give good protection against the cold, even if they are relatively short, but in the case of the Devon and Cornish Rexes and the Sphynx, their sparse coat coverings mean that owners tend to keep them indoors rather than allowing them to roam over long distances.

BREEDS AND ACTIVITY LEVELS

Naturally active breeds include the Maine Coon and Norwegian Forest Cat, both of which are farm cats in origin, and the Turkish Van, which is a village cat that likes to swim. Renowned home-loving cats include the Persian Longhair and Ragdoll, while the Sphynx and Cornish and Devon Rexes tend to be kept in the home because of their sparse coats.

Hunting

A major activity of cats that are allowed to wander outside is hunting, even if they rarely stray far from the garden. Hunting provides both physical and mental exercise, and is unlikely to be a source of excess calories because most domestic cats do not eat what they catch. Furthermore, their hunting attempts are frequently unsuccessful, and in many cases they are not even pitting their skills against live quarry. Domestic cats often pursue inanimate objects, particularly leaves that are blowing about in the garden.

If a cat does catch a live creature, the cat is often incapable of killing it. Although domestic cats instinctively recognize their prey, they do not know how to kill it unless they have been taught to do so by their mother before they were weaned. Even if they do kill their prey, the food may need to be prepared before it can be eaten, and again this appears not to be an instinctive skill. While wild cats swallow mice whole, head first so that the mouse does not become stuck in the cat's throat, they invariably scratch off the feathers before attempting to eat a bird. In contrast, most domestic cats have not learned this behaviour, so they may simply hide the bird instead of trying to eat it. This behaviour mimics that of wild cats, which will conceal the remains of a kill that they have not eaten in its entirety, intending to return when they are hungry again.

Cats that have the opportunity to hunt are likely to be fitter than house-bound cats and less vulnerable to obesity as a result. If your cat is house-bound, it is vital to ensure that it still receives the physical and mental stimulation it needs to stay fit and healthy.

The hunting instinct is strong, even in domestic cats, which enjoy the thrill of the chase but rarely eat their kill.

WARNING BELLS

You can reduce the likelihood of your cat catching live prey by fitting your pet with an elasticated collar with a bell attached to it. The idea is that the bell sounds as the cat rushes after its prey, giving the creature more time to escape from the danger. Cats often learn to adapt to this hunting handicap, however, by moving very quietly through undergrowth so that the sound of the bell will not be triggered until the very last minute.

PROTECTING POND LIFE

- Keep your pond netted, especially in the spring when the fish are spawning.
- Incorporate a dense border of marginal plants to make it harder for your cat to reach the water, and therefore the fish.
- Leave the grass long around the edge of the pond when frogs and toads are spawning, so that the young amphibians are less conspicuous when they emerge from the water. Placing large stones around the edge with plants growing around them will make it harder for a cat to catch frogs.
- Place an ultrasonic deterrent next to the pond. This produces a noise that is inaudible to our ears, but that may help to keep a cat out of this area of the garden.

House-Bound Cats

The phenomenon of house cats is contributing to the rising level of obesity seen in the feline population today. The term "house cat" does not refer to a particular breed or group of cats, but is used to indicate a cat that lives permanently indoors rather than being allowed to wander outside. This situation has arisen because of understandable fears about allowing cats out on to the street. However, house-bound cats take less exercise than if they were allowed outdoors, having far less opportunities to climb, jump and explore.

In view of the cat's natural level of activity, it is perhaps not surprising that cats that live permanently indoors are approximately 40 per cent more likely to be obese than those that are allowed to venture outside. This is a reflection of their overall level of activity, because cats wandering outdoors are only likely to sleep for about 13 hours a day, compared with their indoor counterparts who typically spend up to 16 hours asleep. Much of this difference is accounted for by the fact that outdoor cats spend much of their time searching for prey. Catching prey actually represents an inefficient use of energy for domestic cats, because even an experienced hunter is only likely to make a successful kill once in every 10–15 attempts on average. This means that during the course of a day, a domestic cat seeking its own food would need to make over 100 attempts to meet its 300 kcal food requirements.

Cats living permanently indoors are far less active, unless they are encouraged to take more exercise by their owners. Aside from sleeping more, they will tend to fill their time by grooming themselves for longer periods. The downside of this is that they are more likely to swallow loose hairs and suffer from a higher incidence of hairballs as a result. Free-ranging cats only moult seasonally, rather than losing their coat throughout the year, which is a reflection of the lighting and especially the lack of temperature variation in the average home.

Furthermore, they expend less energy on maintaining their body temperature, another factor that predisposes them to weight gain. Left alone for long periods with little to do other than eat, house-bound cats are likely to become bored, which encourages them not just to eat more, but their lower level of activity in turn

House-bound cats sleep longer than those with access to the outside world, owing to boredom and lack of stimulation.

encourages weight gain if their food intake is not curtailed.

If your cat lives indoors permanently, part of the answer will be to create a more interesting environment to stimulate your pet to move around more. This can be achieved with just minor changes. For example, you could try moving your cat's food to a new location in the home, so that the cat has to walk to another part of the house to eat rather than take just a few steps from where it has been sleeping. Your cat will soon realize where to find the food and adapt accordingly, particularly if you place your pet near the food for the first few mealtimes after moving the bowl. However, you do not want your cat simply to take up residence by the bowl's new location, so do not make the area too cosy. If previously you kept the bowl in a warm part of the kitchen, for example, you could try moving it to a utility room, or another area away from the warmth of the oven.

A more ambitious option is to construct an outdoor cattery where your pet will be safe during the day, while taking more exercise than if it were housed permanently indoors, especially if you incorporate climbing areas into the design (see chapter 8 for further details).

MOULTING AND HAIRBALLS

Cats that spend much of their time roaming outdoors on a daily basis are more likely to display natural moulting cycles than those living permanently indoors, which may shed their hair almost constantly. The natural cycle involves two major periods of moulting each year, starting in the autumn. This is when they are more likely to be vulnerable to hairballs, caused by loose hairs becoming stuck on the cat's rough tongue during grooming. When swallowed, these hairs form a mass in the cat's stomach.

A cat suffering from a hairball will appear to have become fussy about its food, eating smaller quantities than normal while returning much more regularly to the food bowl, sometimes appearing almost constantly hungry. This is because the cat cannot eat as much as normal because of the mat of fur in its stomach.

Regular daily brushing is essential for long-haired cats in order to reduce the risk of hairballs by removing much of the loose hair from the coat. Furthermore, a food that contains components specially formulated to help to protect against blockages in the digestive tract arising from hairballs is to be recommended.

Safety Considerations

There are a number of reasons why cats should not be let out to roam freely. Much depends on where you live, and the level of traffic in the vicinity. There is also the possibility of theft to consider, especially if you have a pure-bred cat. One of the most worrying and potentially upsetting aspects of allowing cats out is the fact that a few disappear and are never seen again, in spite of every effort on the part of the owner to trace the missing pet.

If you do decide to allow your cat out to roam, you can minimize the risks to your pet in a number of ways. Firstly, only allow your cat out during the day, because cats are at greater risk of being involved in traffic accidents after dark. This is partly due to their eyesight (see page 41), but also because drivers fail to see them in the dark and may be driving faster at night, when the roads are less congested. There is also less traffic noise at night, so cats are more likely to venture out into the road than they would be during the day.

As an additional precaution, you may want to fit your pet with an elasticated reflective collar. The collar will reflect the light from the vehicle's headlamps and alert a driver to your pet's presence in the road. You can also attach a capsule to the collar, with a piece of paper inside on which you have written your phone number. This will enable anyone who finds your cat to contact you if there has been an accident or if your cat has simply strayed.

Since cats do lose their collars, it can also be worthwhile having your pet microchipped. The microchip, about the size of a grain of rice, contains a unique code. It is implanted using a syringe-like tool under the cat's skin at the back of the neck. If your cat is then handed in to a rescue organization, they will check with a special reader to see if the cat is microchipped, and will be able check against a central database of microchip numbers and owners' details so that you can be reunited with your pet.

There is less that you can do to protect your cat from becoming involved in fights. You may not be immediately aware that your cat has been involved in a fight, until an abscess starts to develop. This will rapidly form a large swelling, and feel warm to the touch. You may notice the two canine puncture wounds left by the other cat's teeth, which injected the unpleasant bacteria under the skin. Bathing the abscess with warm salt water is recommended, to bring it to a head, but it may need to be drained by a vet. Your cat may develop a slight fever because of this infection, so a course of antibiotics is often needed, and the cat may also go off its food for a time. There is also the risk of the bite transferring viral infections such as feline leukaemia and feline AIDS.

The risk of your cat becoming involved in fights is a good reason for neutering your cat, because a neutered cat is less likely to become involved in a fight when out in the neighbourhood. The risk of aggressive encounters becomes relatively slight, and certainly should not deter you from letting your cat out to exercise in areas where it is safe to do so.

Territories

Cats that have to cover a wide area to catch prey expend more energy and will be correspondingly fitter than those confined to the home or an outdoor cattery in the garden. Male cats have a significantly larger territorial range than female cats, varying anywhere in the region of 0.4–990 hectares. Females may cover an area as small as 0.02 hectares, and rarely exceed 170 hectares. Within this territory there tends to be a core area where a cat spends most of its time, typically covering 0.1–0.45 hectares.

This means that a female is a better choice of pet if you intend to keep your cat permanently indoors, because she is naturally inclined to occupy a smaller area of territory. Even so, keeping a cat confined in a small apartment, perhaps just 60 sq m (72 sq yds), provides far less opportunity for exercise than would be the case if the cat could wander freely outdoors.

As a consequence, it is important to enrich a house cat's environment with plenty of toys, climbing frames and similar items. Otherwise, cut off from other cats and with little to do, it is hardly surprising that a cat will become bored and less active as a result, which in turn triggers weight gain.

One solution is to keep more than one cat in the home on a permanent basis, so that they can occupy each other when you are out. However, it can often be difficult to introduce a second cat successfully alongside an established individual once your existing pet is already settled in your home. Suddenly presenting a newcomer can lead to undesirable behaviours on the part of your established pet. Regarding the new arrival as a territorial incursion, your existing pet may spray the house in an attempt to reassert its authority and reinforce its territorial claims. Hopefully, this phase will quickly pass, but there is no guarantee that the cats will get along and play with each other. Indeed, they may spend their time avoiding each other instead.

If you are thinking of acquiring a cat to live indoors on a permanent basis, you should seriously consider choosing two kittens together at the outset, rather than just one. It will help if they are littermates, because they will be socialized with each other already. A kitten that has grown up in a relatively large litter, in a house full of cats, is likely to be more social than a kitten that has been reared in isolation, even if you want to introduce another kitten to it rather than a littermate. This is because there is a key period in a kitten's development, between three and six weeks of age, when it learns how to react to others of its kind. This is why feral kittens, growing up as part of a colony of cats, remain social with their own kind but are unlikely to be friendly towards people, because they will not have been exposed to humans at this early stage in life.

Two kittens from the same litter make ideal playmates and will keep each other occupied, even when confined indoors.

PROMOTING EXERCISE

Indoors
- Give your cat access to as many rooms as possible so that your pet can roam around.
- Encourage your cat to follow you around the home when going about day-to-day activities.
- Leave plenty of toys lying around. This will remind you to play with your cat, giving your pet brief bursts of exercise.
- Train your cat to come to you when you call its name.
- Keep windowsills free of ornaments and houseplants. This will encourage your pet to jump up and look outside, providing physical and mental stimulation.

Outdoors
- Make sure that your pet is not too scared to go out into the garden; patch up fences if neighbours' cats are invading the territory and scaring your cat off.
- Spend time outdoors in the garden with your pet if it is safe to do so.
- Leave toys, especially small balls, lying around the garden for your cat to play with.
- Place a pile of logs or old wood in the garden that your cat can use as a scratching post and territory marker.
- Make sure that there is a safe area high up to which your cat can escape, and that is not accessible from other gardens.

Creative Play

It is likely that your pet is very familiar with the layout of the rooms in your home, especially if your cat lives permanently indoors. As well as changing your pet's diet, it is also important to raise its level of interest and therefore activity by changing its surroundings. This does not require a large investment. Cats often love to explore cardboard boxes, for example. You may have a large box already, or can acquire one quite easily,

for your pet to play with. Cut out one of the ends and then incorporate the box into games when you are playing with your cat. Roll a ball or aim a clockwork mouse so that it disappears into the box, to encourage your cat to venture inside after

Provide your cat with a selection of simple toys and play games together on a regular basis.

the toy. Alternatively, cut a flap in opposite ends of the box, so that the box acts as a tunnel through which the cat has to chase the toy. Your pet may jump up on top of the box, so it is important that it is secure enough to support your cat's weight.

Large paper shopping bags are also ideal for keeping a cat's interest. Your pet may venture into the bag after a toy, grabbing and bringing it out. Once such items are damaged, they can be replaced easily. You may want to build a more complex network of tunnels for your cat, by joining a number of boxes and bags together. This instinctively appeals to cats, whose wild relatives will invariably hide away in small caves and burrows. The advantage of this type of arrangement is that it can be changed easily and cheaply on a regular basis, which is likely to appeal to the investigative side of your cat's nature. If you want to make the boxes complement the decor in the room, simply stick wrapping paper around them.

AVOIDING BOREDOM

It is important in the context of a cat's overall health to ensure that your pet remains active and does not become bored around the home. This is not just significant in relation to weight loss, but also to long-term mental health. Cats can suffer from a range of behavioural problems linked with boredom. The most self-evident is if your pet refuses to settle down at night and appears restless, although this can be a reflection of the weather. Cats in general are very sensitive to the approach of thunderstorms, and they often start behaving in this way when a storm is imminent, becoming increasingly distressed. More sinister behavioural problems linked with boredom can include excessive grooming, and sometimes displays of aggression towards people.

Hopefully your cat will play by itself when you are out during the day, but there are a number of different things you can do to encourage such behaviour. Technology can be used to help keep your cat alert and active. Some cats like to sit and watch images on television or computer screens. Special DVDs to entertain cats are now being marketed, but you may find that a general DVD will hold your cat's interest just as well. A cat may also find the background chatter and music provided by a radio of comfort, staying awake for longer than when left at home without this stimulus.

Play Gyms

Play gyms are available for cats. These activity centres provide a cat with the opportunity to explore, hide away, climb and paw at toys,

Cats love exploring new objects and will spend hours playing in 'play gyms', or even in ordinary cardboard boxes and paper bags.

GROOMING AND EXERCISE

Playing with your cat is not the only way to keep your pet active. Regular grooming is also useful for this purpose. Cats usually enjoy this experience in any case, and will roll around quite happily while you groom them; this also helps to tone up their muscles, and keeps them fitter as a result. In the case of long-haired cats, grooming is particularly important, because obese individuals are often unable to bend and groom themselves easily. This leaves them at greater risk of developing mats in their coat.

mimicking the natural activity patterns that your pet would indulge in outdoors. These units can be expensive to purchase, so be sure to choose one that is durable and well built. Ideally, the design needs to be flexible, allowing you to swap the components around to maintain your cat's level of interest in this type of toy. Cats are innately curious, so rearranging the components will almost inevitably encourage your pet to show increased interest in the play centre again, even if this means purchasing add-on units.

You could try placing a toy impregnated with catnip into the gym, or even put some sprigs of this herb on top of the unit to encourage your pet to climb up (see pages 89–90). Although an overweight cat may not be inclined to play at first, you should soon notice that your cat's level of activity increases as it starts to lose weight, particularly if you encourage playing. Before long, you may find that your cat actively seeks you out to play, rather like a dog, which is the ideal situation. This will reinforce the bond between you and your pet, but it will also help to ensure that your cat receives regular exercise, which is very important in terms of weight loss.

Cats generally do not want to play for long spells, but instead prefer a series of short games throughout the day. This reflects their normal level of activity; when they are out hunting, they are active in short bursts, rather than remaining active for two or three hours at a time. Do not be surprised if your cat has only a limited interest in playing at first, especially if it is not used to regular exercise. This simply reflects the fact that your cat is not used to a high level of activity and is unfit; its activity levels will increase dramatically as weight loss progresses, making playing easier.

Always begin a game slowly, giving the cat a few minutes to warm up its muscles in order to avoid the risk of injury. As it starts to become more active, the cat is likely to lose weight with greater ease as the weeks pass.

Self-Build Gyms

Depending on the space that you have available in your home or garden, and your carpentry skills, you can construct your own activity centre for your cat, based on your own design. This has the added advantage of being able to fill the space that you have available, perhaps running alongside a wall rather than protruding into the room itself. Even if you are not sufficiently confident to build this yourself, it should not be difficult to find a carpenter who can undertake this task for you.

If you want your cat to climb, provide a ramp leading up to a play box. This can simply be a plank that will give your cat easy access. You could also connect a ramp to a sleeping box in the form of a cube measuring about 40cm (15in), with another ramp behind to help your cat back down again to the ground. You must ensure that the edges of the timber are smooth, so that there is no risk of your cat acquiring splinters in its pads. Also make sure that the design is stable and will not tip over as your cat climbs around. Provided that there is sufficient space available, the unit may extend to several levels in height.

One of the drawbacks of some commercially available cat gyms is the soft material used in their design. This can encourage the spread of fleas, which are difficult if not impossible to remove.

Construct an activity centre for your cat: this can include a ramp, different levels, or just a simple scratching post with a toy attached.

If your cat gym is held together with screws and brackets, you will be able to take it apart easily in order to scrub the components clean, minimizing the risk of the unit becoming unhygenic. Loose bedding can be washed regularly, or even discarded if it becomes badly spoiled. Rather than looking at bare wood, you can paint part of the gym, such as the sleeping box, but obviously ensure that the paint is not toxic to cats, and keep your pet away until the paint has dried thoroughly.

You may also decide to incorporate a scratching post at ground level, which may be one of the vertical supports of the structure. Simply bind the post with sisal rope. Another option is to incorporate toys that will attract your cat to climb up to play, even in your absence. A modified fishing pole, with a coloured feather attached to the end, for example, can attract your cat to play with it when it moves in a draught or when your cat brushes past.

Cat Toys

When it comes to choosing toys, there is an ever-increasing number that you can buy at pet stores. Many cats like to chase after toys, so small balls that they can pat along with their paws and also pounce on are very useful. You can roll the ball along the floor for your pet when you are playing together, and your cat may even decide to play with a toy of this type when you are out, especially once it becomes fitter. Clockwork toys, usually in the shape of mice or other prey, are also popular for cats, although your pet obviously cannot play with such toys without your presence.

There are other toys that can help to improve a cat's muscle tone and contribute to its overall level of fitness. Examples include toy fish that dangle from a miniature fishing rod. The idea is that the cat will sit up and swat the fish with its paws. Similar toys made of feathers can be played with in the same way, dangled from a string or twig. Do not expect an overweight cat to sit right

up on its haunches and play with a toy of this type at first. Hold the toy so that it is closer to the ground, enabling your pet to pat at it while sitting normally. As the cat loses weight, it will become more agile and you can raise the toy.

Cats are curious by nature, so be creative in your choice of toys, but be aware that your cat is likely to show some individual preferences that may hark back to the toys your cat played with as a kitten. Cats tend to see toys as prey, and kittenhood is the time when hunting preferences are acquired and learned from the mother. In the same way that some cats prefer to hunt voles rather than rabbits in areas where voles are common, so they may prefer to chase after a ball rather than another type of toy, based on their experiences early in life.

This is not to say that a cat will refuse to play a game with you if you do not use the preferred toy. Rather, it simply reduces the likelihood that the cat will play with the toy in your absence. Before you go out, always put the toy in the same place, and then you will be able to see whether it has moved while you were out, indicating that your cat has been playing with it when alone, which is what you are striving for.

A cat's surroundings may also influence the choice of toy, and how much exercise that the cat gets playing with it. For example, a cat will not be able to pat a ball with its paws for any significant distance across a carpet that has a deep pile, compared with a wooden or tiled floor over which the ball will roll smoothly. As a result, the cat is more likely to lose interest in the ball. If the ball were able to roll some distance away over a smooth surface, your cat would be more likely to chase after it.

Many cat toys are available: you may find that your cat has a favourite or may prefer household items such as an old sock to a shop-bought toy.

HUNTING AND PLAYING

There is a fairly widespread belief that cats cannot be trained like dogs, but it is certainly possible to teach cats to play, just as queens teach their kittens to hunt. This is why playing regularly with cats at an early age means that they are less likely to be sedentary once they grow up, because playing will have become a habit for them. Playing is very similar to hunting, but it provides a cat with exercise while avoiding the less desirable consequences of hunting behaviour.

It is therefore quite possible to reach a situation where a cat will play on its own, because playing is very similar to hunting. The cat will stalk the toy, chase after it and jump on it, just as it would if it were hunting a mouse. The desire to chase prey is

Playing is very similar to hunting and a cat will often stalk a toy and chase after it as if it were hunting a mouse.

instinctive, while the techniques of killing prey have to be learned. However, there is no real evidence that cats recognize or prefer toys shaped like mice, compared with an ordinary small ball, because neither will have the scent of prey attached to it.

The Appeal of Catnip

Many cats display a peculiar fascination with a herb known as catnip or catmint. This becomes very apparent if you have the plant growing in your garden, because you will notice that your pet and probably other cats from the neighbourhood are almost irresistibly drawn to it. They will start by sniffing repeatedly at the leaves, and then may start to nibble at the plant. Soon, you may notice that the cat goes into a trance-like state, and might start rolling around on the ground, appearing very relaxed. Such behaviour usually lasts up to a quarter of an hour, depending on the impact the catnip has on the individual cat.

It is not clear why this plant should be so attractive to cats, and induce such obvious signs

A catnip plant in your garden will lure your pet outdoors into the fresh air where it will find other distractions.

of euphoria. It may be the fact that the active ingredient, a substance called nepetalactone, is similar to marijuana. Another possible explanation is that this chemical might have a similar but more intense odour to that produced in the urine of a tom cat, which encourages a female in heat to relax and roll around on the ground prior to mating. The drawback to this explanation is that catnip has a similar effect on both male and female cats, including queens that are not in heat. On the other hand, its effects are not just confined to domestic cats – wild cats, including tigers, have been shown to be attracted to this plant.

Manufacturers of toys often impregnate them with catnip oil, although the effects of this are less marked than when a cat is sniffing the plant, and its impact is gradually lost over time. In the short term, however, this may serve to draw your cat's attention to the toy, and encourage playing. If your cat is responsive to it, you can encourage a cat outdoors using catnip.

Not all cats respond to catnip, however; it is estimated that somewhere between a half and a third are not affected by it. Young kittens, especially under two months, are likely to be unresponsive to the effects of this herb.

Toys and Your Cat's Routine

Cats will derive most exercise by chasing after toys, rather than patting at a suspended toy with a paw. This latter behaviour can occupy them, however, helping to prevent them from becoming bored when they are alone. This will discourage your pet from sleeping during the daytime, becoming more active as a result. The way in which a cat pats at a toy resembles the way in which some cats find dripping taps fascinating, sitting for hours in some cases, watching the droplets of water fall and often trying to catch them by using one of their paws.

Some toys can only be used when you are at home, such as clockwork mice that need to be wound up and then run over the floor in a haphazard fashion, hopefully being pursued by your pet. Once again, the surface of the floor is

important, because a hard surface will be more suitable for operating these toys.

It is worthwhile trying to link periods of play and feeding whenever possible, again reflecting what would be the natural behaviour of a cat in the wild. In this case, encourage your cat to scamper after a clockwork toy prior to feeding. This is the stage at which a cat is most likely to want to play, rather than after a meal. Your pet's innate hunting instincts will be awakened while hungry, and soon your cat will come to associate chasing after the toy with being fed, seeing it as part of the process.

You may be surprised to discover just how adaptable your cat can be when it comes to developing play habits. Certain breeds, notably the Devon and Cornish Rexes, can sometimes

Encourage your cat to play with toys from an early age to keep its hunting instincts alive as well as its interest in activity and exercise.

display dog-like retrieving behaviour during the course of a game, learning to bring a toy back to the owner.

Cats are nocturnal by nature, because this is when their natural prey, rodents, emerge from their hiding places and can be caught most easily. However, they do adapt their lifestyle when living as pets to be similar to that of their owners, particularly cats that live permanently indoors. It will therefore do no harm to wake a cat up and encourage it to play during the daytime, particularly because indoor cats sleep longer than their free-roaming counterparts anyway.

Always remember that the aim is to slim down your cat, so do not reward your pet regularly with treats during the course of a game. This is not just unnecessary, but also counterproductive. Treats are often laden with calories, and could prevent a cat from losing weight despite increasing its level of activity. Praise and stroke your pet by all means, although most cats are not overtly affectionate during play, preferring to concentrate on the game itself at this stage. If you feel bad about not rewarding your pet, this is another good reason to play before a mealtime, so that you still feel that you are treating your cat.

DANGEROUS ITEMS

Some items are dangerous for cats to play with. Glass balls of any kind, such as those used to decorate Christmas trees, are potentially hazardous, because they can break and shards of glass could easily injure a cat's foot; any cut across the pads in particular will bleed profusely. Avoid using small beads or similar items as cat toys, because your pet could swallow them and they might form an obstruction in the throat, causing the cat to choke. Plastic bags are also dangerous.

Do not use a woollen item as a lure to encourage your cat to pounce on it, because the fibres could easily become wrapped around the cat's teeth. String is safer, but fibres may work loose and could cause choking if the fibres become stuck at the back of the throat.

Any toys that contain sharp objects, such as staples or paper clips, are also a threat to your pet's health, and check that there are no exposed nails or screws in any cat furniture that you buy or make. A good rule of thumb with toys that are not specially designed for cats is to check whether they are approved for use with young children, making them also suitable for use with a cat.

CATS AND GRASS

If your cat is used to eating fresh grass, do not try to stop this behaviour. A number of owners whose cats live indoors permanently provide this to their pets in the form of special trays. It can be grown easily on a windowsill from kits that are available in many pet stores, and you can allow your pet to help itself, although take care to ensure that furniture sprays and similar chemicals cannot contaminate the grass in the room. This greenstuff will add to your cat's fibre intake, but will not raise the calorie count. Do not be tempted to use ordinary lawn grass seed, because this is often treated with chemicals that could be harmful to your pet. As an alternative, you can grow millet seeds sold for birds.

If your cat suddenly starts eating more grass than normal, it could indicate that your pet has a hairball, which is likely to be vomited up in due course, with the grass serving as an emetic. Cats that wander freely outside may also eat grass if they have a heavy infestation of parasitic worms.

The growing of catnip and grass indoors can also have other benefits, if they are positioned in such a way that the cat has to climb in order to reach them. By stimulating the cat's interest, your pet can be lured to jump up onto windowsills or explore different areas of the house. This encourages your pet to increase its level of activity, which is especially important for house-bound and overweight cats.

Cats often eat grass to help dislodge a hairball. If you grow grass indoors, position the tray on a windowsill so that your cat has to jump up to reach it.

Medical Problems

As your cat progresses from kitten to elderly feline, there are a number of occasions when weight gain could become an issue. Obesity can be the result or the cause of a variety of medical problems, so it is important to take preventative measures before it occurs if possible. Kittens are very lively, and as a result they are unlikely to become overweight, even if they are living permanently in the home. However, this situation may not continue: studies have shown that cats kept indoors are 40 per cent more likely to be obese, compared to those that can roam outdoors as well. You need to be aware that bad habits acquired at an early stage could easily contribute to your cat becoming fat in the future.

It can be very difficult to ignore the plaintive meowing of a young kitten, but once you have provided a tidbit, you will soon become a hostage to fortune, with your cat always hanging around when you are eating. Worse still, you may be giving it morsels of fatty or other inappropriate food that could be detrimental to its health. There is no need to reward a cat or kitten with food, or to use tidbits to gain a cat's attention. Simply calling your pet to you should evoke a response, if the cat knows that you will make a fuss of it or play a game. Once your cat has matured, it will be advisable to get it neutered. Neutering doubles a cat's life expectancy on average, but it does carry an associated risk of weight gain.

Neutering and Weight Gain

Neutering can have a dramatic effect in terms of increasing your cat's weight because it induces changes in the body's metabolism. A cat's body weight can increase by 50 per cent within a three-month period after surgery, if the cat is allowed to carry on eating as it did beforehand. It may not just be a question of reducing the total amount of food on offer, but also switching to a brand that has a lower fat content. Fast weight gain of this magnitude places significantly greater demands on both a cat's skeletal frame and its organs, resulting in loss of mobility as well as a risk of disease.

The inevitable loss of agility as a result of this dramatic increase in weight then means that your cat will take less exercise. It marks the start of a downward spiral that sees cats becoming less inclined to climb and jump, or run and chase after toys. As weight gain in cats can arise relatively fast after neutering, you cannot simply rely on an annual visit to your vet for your cat's immunizations to spot that your pet is becoming overweight. Even the six-monthly check-ups that may take place for an elderly cat are too infrequent, because older cats are at particular risk of obesity. Monitor your cat's condition every two weeks after neutering over the course of several months, and then once a month thereafter. Obesity is a problem that will not go away on its own, and can give rise to unexpected complications. Should your pet need emergency surgery, for example, being overweight can increase the risk of complications arising from the anaesthetic. Furthermore, under emergency circumstances, you will have no opportunity to slim down your pet.

GROOMING PROBLEMS

Being obese can affect your cat's daily life in ways quite apart from taking exercise. Overweight cats frequently have difficulty grooming themselves, especially if they are long-haired. This can lead to a matted coat, which in turn may increase the risk of faecal contamination, attracting flies in warm weather.

Abdominal Bloating

Some medical conditions, often serious, may cause a cat's abdomen to swell in size. This is why it is a good idea to arrange a veterinary check-up, before placing your cat on a diet. You can then be certain that there is no underlying medical problem, and this also gives you the opportunity to draw up a weight-loss plan with your vet. Such is the scale of obesity among pets today that many practices often run special clinics to help owners to address this problem.

If your cat puts on a lot of weight suddenly, with its belly becoming swollen, it may be suffering from bloat. This may be directly linked with obesity, because one of the most common causes of bloat is constipation. Constipation is a more frequent problem in overweight cats because the overall muscle tone in their bodies is reduced, and so they are not processing their food effectively. Treatment to relieve the constipation will resolve the immediate discomfort for your cat in this case. Switching to a higher fibre diet may help to prevent a recurrence of the problem, although the longer term solution will be for your pet to lose weight. Old cats are especially prone to becoming constipated, with obesity simply increasing the likelihood that they will develop this condition.

A sudden increase in size of your cat's abdomen may also indicate a urinary obstruction. This is a very serious condition, because if left untreated, the bladder is likely to rupture. Small stones may form in the bladder, and then get swept down the urethra, which leads from the bladder out of the body. The stones ultimately cause an obstruction here, cutting off the flow of urine. Another key indicator of this problem is if your cat hunches when trying to urinate, rather than crouching down, in an attempt to relieve the pain, but with little or no urine emerging.

Long-standing illnesses can resemble weight gain, especially when there is an accumulation of fluid in the cat's abdominal cavity. This is a typical feature of feline infectious peritonitis. Once this infection has gained access to the body, your cat may suffer a transient fever, appearing generally off-colour for a few days, but then appears to recover uneventfully. You may even forget that your pet has been ill, and in some cases there are no initial symptoms whatsoever. Unfortunately , the virus remains within the body and starts to replicate. It attacks the peritoneum – the lining of the abdominal cavity – and there is a build-up of fluid here, known as ascites, that makes the abdomen look swollen.

Heart failure can also result in an accumulation of fluid in the abdominal cavity. A general loss of vitality will also be noted in such cases, which you might otherwise put down to your cat's increased weight. This again emphasizes why it is vital to have your pet examined by a vet. In this case, appropriate medication in the form of tablets should help to resolve the problem.

You will need to determine whether your cat's distended stomach is the result of a long-standing medical condition or simply excess weight.

Rapid Weight Loss

You might think it is a good thing if your overweight cat loses its appetite for a few days, reasoning that this will slim down your pet. Unfortunately, due to one of the quirks in the metabolism of cats, this can actually cause serious illness and even death, whatever the underlying cause of your pet's lack of appetite. This is why, when you change your cat's food for any reason, you need to do so gradually, so as not to deter your pet from eating. Change approximately 30 per cent of your cat's food per week, to encourage it to develop a taste for the new food, without risk to its health (see page 61).

The underlying mechanism behind this problem is unclear, but the result is that the liver ends up being infiltrated by fat in the form of triglycerides, to the extent that it can no longer function effectively. Your cat's weight will fall dramatically, not just because it has lost its appetite, but also because it is likely to be afflicted by vomiting and diarrhoea. One of the most evident indicators may be a yellowing of the white areas of the eyes, and also the pink areas of the mouth. This condition, which is serious, can be confirmed by a blood test.

As an initial step in treatment, your vet is likely to give fluids intravenously to your pet, and it is important to try to persuade the cat to start eating as quickly as possible – sometimes appetite-stimulant drugs are given for this reason. Food may also be given by tube. The amount of food offered is built up over several days, being given frequently in small amounts in order to lessen the strain on the liver and allow it to recover.

Not eating can affect your cat's metabolism, making it lethargic as well as affecting its liver. Treat loss of appetite seriously and seek medical advice.

SCAVENGING PROBLEMS

If your cat is gagging and pawing at its mouth in distress, check that it does not have a bone stuck in its mouth. If your pet is on a diet, it may have scavenged from a dustbin or elsewhere. With one hand on your cat's lower jaw, prise open the upper jaw with the other hand. Wear gloves in case your cat scratches you, and it is worth wrapping the cat in a towel as well. In good light, you might be able to see the bone at the back of the mouth; if you cannot and your cat is in obvious distress, take your pet to the vet to discount the possibility that it may have been bitten or stung by a wasp. Apart from the obvious risk of fish and chicken bones, there is also the possibility that your cat may have ingested old, bacteria-infected food.

Even if your cat vomits up the contaminated food, it may be worth seeking veterinary advice, because you may have to feed your cat a special remedial food before it will return to its original cat food – even if this is not the source of the stomach upset, such is the cat's instinct to survive that it will avoid any of its previous food for fear that this was the cause of the illness. After about six weeks, you should be able to put your cat back on its former diet.

Diabetes

The pancreas may also be affected if your cat changes its diet radically over a short period of time. The pancreas lies quite close to the liver and is attached to the first part of the small intestine, known as the duodenum. There are two parts to the pancreas: one part produces digestive enzymes and the other produces the hormone insulin, which passes into the blood stream. This chemical messenger encourages the cells around the body to take up glucose, providing them with energy.

Unfortunately, in seriously overweight cats the cells in the body become less responsive to insulin, resulting in Type II diabetes. This differs from cases where the actual output of insulin from the pancreas falls, which is described as Type I diabetes. The indications are that Type II diabetes is becoming increasingly common in the feline population as the result of rising levels of obesity, because excess fat interferes with the functioning ability of insulin.

Typical signs of diabetes are an increased appetite and thirst, accompanied by weight loss. This is because although nutrients are being absorbed into the bloodstream, they cannot be utilized by the cells. This results in the breakdown of body fat and the presence of ketone bodies, which are a side-effect of this process and will give a distinctly sickly odour to the cat's breath. If untreated, the cat will continue to deteriorate, and ultimately it will collapse into a coma.

It is usually necessary to offer smaller but more frequent meals to diabetic cats, to avoid significant peaks in the demand for insulin, and to slow down insulin production. Large meals result in a sudden upsurge in demand for this hormone as glucose is absorbed into the bloodstream.

Older cats are especially vulnerable to diabetes, but if you can bring the illness under control, they do not develop the complications seen in humans. Even so, you will need to be prepared to give your pet regular injections of insulin. It is also very important to keep your cat's lifestyle stable; if your cat suddenly increases its activity levels, for example, this will require more energy, which in turn will impact on the insulin levels in the body.

Equally, if a diabetic cat loses its appetite for any reason, it could lapse into a coma as blood sugar levels fall and the cat becomes hypoglycemic. Before this happens, the cat will show signs of loss of co-ordination, tilting its head and appearing very weak, because of the lack of glucose in the bloodstream. You will need to boost the cat's blood sugar by giving it some honey in water. The reaction should be rapid, with your pet appearing normal again within 15 minutes.

The insulin itself needs to be stored in a refrigerator, and handled carefully, to maintain its activity. Injecting a cat with the special fine needle is generally straightforward in most cases, especially once your pet becomes used to the procedure. Your vet will show you how to give the injection, and if you are nervous beforehand, practice with a water-filled syringe and orange.

A cat that is suffering from diabetes will lose weight as part of the illness. It is very important to follow your vet's advice, both to stabilize your cat's condition and manage its weight. There are special diabetic diets available that your vet can prescribe as part of the treatment. These are relatively high in indigestible fibre, so they make the cat feel full, but do not yield as much energy as a regular food. They do not contain the carbohydrate found in most normal cat foods, which cats do not actually need (as true carnivores, the cat's metabolism is geared towards processing protein and fat). The use of these new foods has actually meant that in some cases, regular diabetic injections have no longer proved to be necessary, especially if the cat has also lost weight.

Slimming down a diabetic cat, however, is something that needs to be undertaken strictly on the basis of veterinary advice, to avoid possible complications. It is especially important not to allow the cat to stray in search of other food, which will interfere both with the diet and treatment, having potentially serious consequences. You may therefore need to curtail your cat's ability to roam, and you must not offer any treats either.

OLD AGE AND CATS

Cats may live for 20 years or more, with the stages of their life being divided as follows:
Kitten: Up to 18 months, depending on the breed. Large breeds such as Persians mature significantly later than oriental breeds such as the Burmese and Siamese, which may be sexually mature by 4–6 months old.
Adult: From the end of kittenhood up to 7 years of age.
Senior: 7–13 years old.
Elderly: 13 years onwards.

Most cat food manufacturers recommend transferring a cat to a senior diet from the age of seven years. This has fewer calories than a standard ration, as appropriate for an older cat that has become less energetic, and contains ingredients such as antioxidants to help slow down the aging process. Senior diets are also carefully formulated to take account of the declining function of organ systems such as the kidneys, which is an inevitable accompaniment of old age.

Genetic Abnormalities

An extremely rare situation where weight gain might be genetic in origin has been reported in the case of male tortoiseshell cats. Tortoiseshell coloration normally only occurs in female cats because their sex chromosomes are of even length, designated XX. What distinguishes males genetically is that one of the chromosomes on which genes are located, is shorter than the other.

Always feed your cat food appropriate to its age. Once it is seven years old, a 'senior' diet will be more suited to its nutritional requirements.

This is known as the Y chromosome, with males therefore having an XY genotype.

There is an exceedingly rare condition where a male cat inherits an additional X chromosome, so that its genetic make-up is XXY. This accounts for its tortoiseshell coloration, although the presence of the additional X chromosome also means that the cat will be infertile. In humans, as well as cats, this condition is known as Klinefelter's syndrome, named after the doctor who identified it. A similar condition in female cats is called XXX syndrome, but is less documented because it is not evident from a cat's coat coloration and gender.

Kittens born with an extra sex chromosome are often smaller than normal at birth, appearing as the runts of the litter, but they are likely to grow more quickly than their littermates. They frequently become taller, and in a few cases the condition appears to lead to weight gain.

The best-documented example is a cat called Brody, who was adopted as a kitten in the mid-1990s by his owner Laura Baker of Dublin, Ohio, in the United States. A male cat with tortoiseshell and white patterning, Brody also had misshapen hind feet, and was not expected to live long because of his Klinefelter's syndrome, although this prediction proved incorrect. Brody's weight increased markedly after the age of two, reaching more than 11 kg (25 lb) by the time he was seven years old – his owner described him as the size of a small sheep at this stage.

Metabolic Disturbances

An inactive thyroid, known as hypothyroidism (not to be confused with the overactive thyroid condition known as hyperthyroidism), is sometimes blamed for weight gain. However, this is an exceedingly rare condition, and in fact cats affected by hypothyroidism do not necessarily suffer from an increase in weight, although they may be less active and will feel the cold.

Hypothyroidism did, however, account for the massive weight gain of what may well be the heaviest cat documented in North America. Spice was a red and white tom living in Ridgefield, Connecticut. He grew to a massive 19.5 kg (43 lb), although he had slimmed down to 15.8 kg (35 lb) by the time of his death, three years later. A thyroid supplement helped Spice to lose weight, after his condition had been diagnosed by a blood test. Treatment for hypothyroidism is straightforward, consisting of tablets to speed up the cat's metabolism. The cat should start to show signs of weight loss within two weeks. The results can be improved by placing the cat on a diet.

Slimming a Cat for Surgery

In the case of an emergency, your vet will have to go ahead and operate regardless of your cat's weight, but the anaesthetic risk is increased in the case of a cat that is seriously overweight, because body organs such as the heart will be working under increased strain. A careful assessment of the cat's overall state of health beforehand will be helpful in terms of highlighting any particular problems, but it will not eliminate the danger. Assuming that all goes well during surgery, the post-operative period is often more difficult for an obese cat. It can be difficult to keep sutures in place if abdominal surgery is involved, while the risk of sores if your cat has to be immobilized for any period of time will also be increased.

If your cat is overweight and you know that it is going to need surgery at some stage, it is therefore particularly important to follow your vet's advice about slimming down your cat. This will ensure that your pet is in the best possible condition for the operation.

Even if your cat has undergone surgery, resist the urge to give it extra treats as this could cause weight-gain, especially if your cat needs to be kept confined.

Fit For Life

It actually takes very little weight gain for a cat to become clinically obese. Obesity is defined as any figure that is at least 15 per cent above a cat's ideal weight. This means that a cat that should weigh 4.5 kg (10 lb) will be clinically obese at just 5.2 kg (11.5 lb). The first thing you need to do is determine how much weight your cat needs to lose. There are safe limits for weight loss, because cats are at risk from hepatic lipidosis (see page 98) if they lose weight too quickly. As a guide, a cat should not lose more than 3 per cent of its body weight each week. It is advisable to change your pet's food to a weight-loss ration in the short term, or to reduce the amount of food by about a third on a daily basis. By a combination of cutting back the calories that your pet is receiving, and increasing the amount of exercise, your cat should soon start to lose weight.

Increasing the amount of exercise that your cat gets
by taking it out into the garden and encouraging play
will help to maintain weight loss.

Keep a Record

Accurate record-keeping forms a vital part of the dieting procedure, although this can easily be overlooked. Keeping a record is the best way to measure your cat's progress, and it can help you to identify factors that may be slowing the process. Start a weight-loss diary on a weekend, when you will have more time available, because you will need to weigh your pet regularly each week. Always do this before you feed your cat in the morning, so that you have a consistent figure while your cat has an empty stomach.

Note down your cat's weight, and then calculate how much your pet should weigh at the end of the following week. Obtain this figure by subtracting 3 per cent from your cat's current weight. It will be easier to work out the percentages in grams rather than pounds and ounces. For example, if a cat weighs 10,000 g (or 10 kg = 22.046 lb), its weight should fall by 3 per cent, which is 300 g. The cat should therefore weigh 9,700 g (or 9.7 kg/21½ lb) at the end of the first week. As the cat's weight falls, the amount that it should lose each week will decline accordingly, so do not be disheartened.

You also need to realize that it will take weeks if not months for your cat to reach its target weight. Sometimes your cat will not lose as much weight as you anticipate, but provided that the weight is going down progressively, this is fine. If the cat loses very little weight over the course of several weeks, however, you need to investigate what is going wrong. The most likely explanation is that your cat is scavenging food elsewhere.

Taking On an Overweight Cat

If you visit a cattery where there are unwanted cats seeking homes, you will see a number of older cats there, because most people are in search of kittens. However, older cats that have been used to living in the home as much-loved pets can settle easily into new surroundings, and can become marvellous companions. However, in a number of cases they may be overweight, and slimming down a new cat can present a particular challenge.

The first thing to do is to have your new cat's health checked out by a vet. Although it will be obvious that a tom has been neutered, it can be harder to determine this in the case of a queen, because the scar will no longer be apparent. Even if you plan to allow your new pet outside in due course, you will need to keep the cat indoors for at least two weeks, so that it can become familiar with its new home and will be less tempted to

If you adopt an overweight cat, make sure it receives a thorough veterinary check before you embark on a programme of weight loss.

stray as a result. What you do not want to do is to place your new cat on a restricted diet, because a hungry cat will have the urge to wander in search of food, which is a particular problem in a new area, where there could be potential dangers.

Start by weighing your new pet, then set up a weight-loss diary to monitor the cat's progress. Spend as much time as possible with your cat during the time that it must stay indoors, building up the bond between you. Cats do learn to recognize their names, so it is not a good idea to try to change your new pet's name from the one that it is already accustomed to. Call the cat to you regularly when you are feeding it, so that your pet learns to identify with you. You can introduce some aspects of dieting right from the outset, by replacing some of your cat's usual food with a lower calorie alternative.

It is also a good idea to increase the number of feeds, dividing up the daily ration of food.

DRAW A WEIGHT-LOSS CHART

Draw up a weight-loss chart for your cat based on a 3 per cent weekly weight-loss goal. Use a sheet of graph paper and put weight on the vertical axis and the number of weeks on the horizontal axis. Divide the vertical axis into 100g units (perhaps one square on the graph could equal 100 g), with your cat's target weight at the bottom and its starting weight at the top of the axis. Start the horizontal axis at the date of the first weigh-in, then divide it into weekly units (again, one square on the graph could equal one week).

Plot the weight of your cat at the outset, then take it down in weekly incremental stages to the ideal weight, using the 3 per cent weekly weight-loss guideline. Plot each weekly target with a cross, then join the crosses with a line to see the target weight-loss progression. Over the weeks, the slope of the line will start to flatten out, because the amount of weight that should be lost will decrease progressively.

Using a different colour, plot your cat's actual weekly weight and check it against the planned weight-loss progression. Plotting the figures on a chart in this way can be encouraging, because you will be able to see very clearly just how much progress your pet is making, and even predict when your cat is likely to reach its target weight. Do not worry too much if your cat does not always lose the target amount, as long as the line of actual weight loss gradually comes down.

By the time that your new pet can be allowed out safely, it will be used to this feeding routine and is less likely to stray because it will know that food is available throughout much of the day (see page 62).

Groom your new cat regularly, because this will build up a bond between you. Try to promote fitness by playing with the cat at every opportunity; this will have the added advantage of helping your pet to integrate into its new home. You can easily establish a regular exercise session

Make every effort to create a good bond with a new pet; you will then find it easier to motivate your cat to respond to you and to exercise when encouraged.

with your pet in this way, but keep the sessions relatively short, so that you do not overtire your pet and cause it to wander off, having lost interest. Also, encourage other members of the family to play with the new cat, as well as participate in keeping the weight-loss diary.

PERSUADING AN OLDER CAT TO PLAY

Cats retain an instinct to play throughout their lives, so it should not be difficult to find a game that appeals even to an old cat. The key in this case is not to expect your pet to be as athletic as when younger. Older cats are less likely to want to climb, for example, but they are usually keen to maintain their reflexes by jumping on or running after toys.

If you adopt an older cat that is overweight, there is a possibility that your new pet may not be used to playing. You may have to coax him into playing, especially if he is nervous by nature. Perhaps the most important thing is to start when you have plenty of time and the home is quiet, so that your cat will be relatively relaxed. Begin by making a fuss of your cat, and then gently dangle a toy with a brightly coloured feather attached within easy reach of your cat's front paws. Hopefully before too long, your pet will start to try to reach out to the toy. Do not react by pulling it away, but allow your cat to gain confidence by exploring the toy with its paw. Later, you can hold the toy farther away.

When it comes to ball games, wait until your cat is on the floor. Once again, start by stroking and relaxing your pet. Then gently roll the ball towards your cat's paws from just a short distance away. If your pet ignores the ball initially, spend a few more moments making a fuss of your pet, before rolling the ball past its paws again. Do not roll the ball directly at the cat, because it is likely to get upset if the ball hits it. You may have to repeat this several times before your cat strikes out with its paw at the ball, indicating an interest in playing. Simply carry on rolling the ball past your pet in either direction.

Once the cat is tapping the ball regularly, you can try rolling the ball past your pet from behind, which should encourage the cat to chase the ball. If you play with your cat on a regular daily basis, this will serve to reinforce the bond between you, as well as helping to ensure that your pet becomes fitter, which is an important aspect of any weight-loss programme.

Even a very sedentary elderly cat can usually be encouraged to use its front paws to try to catch a thick piece of rope dragged across the floor within reach. Build on this base by gently flicking a ping-pong ball towards your cat, in the hope that your pet will flick the ball with its paw, and may then react by chasing after it. Each cat has individual preference in terms of play, so you need to experiment to find what is the best type of toy for your pet.

Multi-Cat Households

It can be hard to keep one cat on a successful diet if it shares your home with two or more other cats. Although it is sometimes suggested that it is a

Introducing a kitten into the household may encourage your cat to be more active, but it may also create territorial problems as your cat tries to assert itself.

FIT FOR LIFE

good idea to get another cat, especially a young kitten, as a way of encouraging an existing pet to take more exercise and so lose weight, this can create a number of practical difficulties.

In the first instance, there is no guarantee that the cats will get along. The best way of ensuring compatibility between cats is to start off with two littermates that have grown up together. An older individual that has become used to its territory may well react in an undesirable way, even aggressively, to any incursion by another cat. Your existing pet may also start soiling randomly around the home as a way of reasserting territorial dominance in the face of the perceived challenge by the other cat. This applies irrespective of your original pet's gender, or that of the new cat.

Obtaining another cat is therefore something that needs to be undertaken with careful thought, because it can simply create more difficulties than it solves, especially if your life is already busy. There are significant extra costs and responsibilities involved, in terms of food, veterinary bills and holiday care. If you do decide to go ahead, a kitten is less likely to be perceived as a threat to your existing pet. However, you will need to supervise them carefully, especially at first, because there is no guarantee that the young cat will not be attacked by its established companion.

Littermates are more likely to play well together than cats introduced at a later stage.

The most important thing, in terms of avoiding conflict, is to reinforce the status of your existing pet at every opportunity, rather than paying more attention to the newcomer. If you are playing with your existing pet, do not break off if the other cat comes up to you, but continue giving attention to your established companion. It is also important not to force them together, by holding one in each arm at the same time, for example. Apart from anything else, this could easily end up with you being badly scratched if they both start struggling and squabbling. Hopefully, the cats will gradually accept each other over the course of time.

Acquiring a second cat is certainly not a short-term solution to aiding weight loss, and can actually be counterproductive. This applies especially in the case of a kitten, if your existing cat can steal the kitten's food. This is actually worse than allowing the overweight cat to continue eating its own food, because kitten foods have a higher calorific content than either adult or senior diets. You therefore need to be diligent in ensuring that the cats are fed separately, because an adult cat will not hesitate to steal food from a smaller, weaker companion. This will wreck any progress that you have made in slimming down your existing pet, and might even lead to more weight gain.

The main positive aspect, as far as weight loss is concerned, is that having a kitten in the home is likely to encourage your existing cat to be more lively and active. The kitten will probably want to play with the older companion, and even if the kitten's attempts are rebuffed, this will disrupt your established pet's sleep pattern. The older cat's natural curiosity is also likely to cause the cat to stay awake longer, watching what its younger companion is doing.

When it comes to introducing a mature cat into the household alongside your existing pet, the likelihood is that they will not play together, but the increased tension will again cause your established cat to remain more alert and active, particularly at first, which may help a weight-loss programme. The other thing to bear in mind if you acquire another cat is that you must make sure that you avoid the pitfalls that led to your existing pet becoming overweight.

Other Pets

Acquiring a puppy may actually be a better solution than getting a kitten when it comes to encouraging increased activity in an overweight cat. This is because a puppy is instinctively more playful, and your cat will have to respond, even if this simply means moving around the home to escape from an exuberant canine companion. Most cats soon adapt to the presence of a dog in the home, and may be more ready to play with a dog than another cat, because they do not perceive the dog as a threat to their status. Even so, you should not acquire a dog of any kind, let alone a puppy, just to help your cat take more exercise – especially if you are living in an apartment with no garden, because dogs cannot be kept satisfactorily in these conditions.

It is also important to choose the type of dog carefully. Some dogs are naturally more aggressive than others, and size is also a significant factor. Dogs that grow to a relatively large size may inadvertently injure a cat if they are playing together. You should also avoid breeds like the pug, Pekingese and others that have short muzzles, because their eyes are more prominent and so are at greater risk of being scratched by the cat's claws in any encounter.

If a dog is not an option, an aquarium can sometimes help to make your cat more interested in its surroundings. This needs to be positioned so that the cat can see the fish clearly, perhaps being able to sit quite close to the tank. The cat is unlikely to cause the fish any harm, but as a precautionary measure you must ensure that the aquarium is securely covered; some cats are not averse to dipping their toes into water, and at the very least this could frighten the fish. The cat is likely to sit and watch the fish swimming around. Birds and small mammals of any kind should not be kept in the same room as a cat, however, because they will cause the cat to become aggressive, being a cat's natural prey.

Puppies are instinctively playful and will certainly ensure that your cat is more active. You should, however, choose the type of dog carefully.

CANINE COMPANIONS

The nature of puppies is such that they are unlikely to be aggressive towards a cat, but they must be carefully supervised together, especially at first. Allow them to get to know each other with minimal interference as far as possible. Especially good breeds to live alongside dogs are British shorthairs, Abyssinians and manx cats.

Staying Slim

This chapter will hopefully encourage you to think more carefully about ways of keeping your cat in shape once it's reached its optimum weight and provide a few new ideas of how to achieve this. It's worth remembering that simple, small adjustments can be just as effective as more involved solutions in maintaining your cat's weight and fitness as long as you are committed to adjusting your approach to your cat's health on a permanent basis.

Once your cat has reached its target weight, it is obviously important not to allow the weight to creep back on. Hopefully, now that you are aware of the problem and how it occurred, you will be on guard for the warning signs of weight gain. As a precaution, it is a good idea to continue weighing

Cats may not want to venture outdoors in winter or during bad weather. Try to encourage indoor play during these times to keep your cat's weight stable.

your pet regularly, perhaps twice a month, and to carry on keeping a weight diary (see page 109). You will then notice very quickly if your cat's weight does start to rise again and will be able to tackle the situation before it gets out of hand.

It is important to note, however, that seasonal changes may have a slight effect on your cat's weight, especially in the case of older cats. In winter most cats, and elderly ones in particular, are less inclined to exercise outdoors and, just like humans, are inclined to put on a little weight. In spring energy levels naturally increase and your cat should return to exploring outdoors. Make adjustments for the seasons and don't expect your cat to follow you outside every time you rush into the garden in winter to do a spot of digging. Instead, try to encourage exercise indoors using toys such as a piece of string or a cardboard box to encourage your cat to play with you when you come back in.

Maintaining an Exercise Routine

There are a number of things that you can do, both in the home and outdoors, to ensure that your cat continues to exercise sufficiently after reaching its target weight. Think about how you can create a more cat-friendly garden, for example, perhaps by planting some fast-growing trees that your cat will enjoy climbing. Now that your cat is leaner and healthier, you should notice

Once your cat has lost weight you may find it returns to more athletic activities such as tree-climbing. Try to encourage this by looking at ways to make your garden more cat friendly.

that your pet has become more active and may start spending more time outoors. Encourage outdoor play by leaving favourite toys outside and by spending more time in the garden yourself – your cat may be happy to join you.

Even a simple wooden plank placed alongside a fence, or a piece of trellis positioned against the wall of your house may prove an interesting development to your cat's environment. Many cats like lying in warm, sunny spots on a roof, where they can sunbathe in relative privacy. If your cat enjoyed climbing to locations of this type in the past, it is likely that it will start revisiting these haunts now that it is slimmer and sufficiently agile to be able to climb again.

If your pet is unable to exercise outdoors alone, for safety or other reasons, it is even more important to monitor your cat's weight carefully and to respond to any signs of a return to weight gain. Re-evaluate the opportunities for play in the home and how much time you are spending with your pet. You may also want to consider supervised activities outside the home such as cat-walking, shows, and agility competitions which do not rely on you having access to a garden (see pages 124 and 130). Alternatively you may want to consider building a cattery (see page 132), if you have the space, to provide a permanent, sheltered spot for your cat to exercise.

Food Matters for Maintenance

After slimming your cat down, be particularly careful about feeding your pet freshly-cooked foods, especially if it is older and also as it ages, even if you have done so in the past. Overfeeding with food of this type can be a major contributor to obesity and will allow the pounds to creep back on. It is much better to rely on the most appropriate formulated food, which will normally be a senior diet in the case of an older cat, in spite of the fact that cats will generally prefer to eat cooked meats whenever possible.

The risks posed by overfeeding with fresh-cooked food were conspicuously displayed in the case of Tiddles, who was adopted as a kitten by the attendant at the ladies' lavatory at Paddington Station in London. Commuters used to drop off prize tidbits such as steak for Tiddles, to the extent that she had her own fridge. Unsurprisingly, attempts to put her on a successful diet proved to be impossible. She ended up weighing 14.5 kg (32 lb) and was barely able to move when she had to be put to sleep in 1983.

Even grosser cats have been recorded, however, indicating what could potentially happen to your pet if it is fed on large amounts of foods that are intended primarily for human consumption. A Russian cat called Katy drew widespread media

The agility of a cat is seriously impeded by being overweight. Giving your cat opportunities for exercise is key to a cat returning to its optimum weight.

attention in 2003 when it emerged that she tipped the scales at approximately 44 lb (20 lb), and had a waist measurement of 68.5 cm (27 in). It is believed that she is the most obese example of a domestic cat ever known, with much of her problem stemming from the fact that she could eat vast quantities of sausages at the rate of 1.5 a minute!

The effects of overfeeding are also evident in the case of a cat from China, reported in February 2006. Now nine years old, he weighs 15 kg (33 lb),

REAL LIFE SUCCESS

George's weight grew significantly from middle-age onwards, largely because his owner insisted on feeding him tidbits and table scraps in addition to generous helpings of his regular food. Nor did she change his diet to a lower calorie senior ration as he aged. It finally reached the point where George tipped the scales at over 8.6 kg (19 lb) and had lost much inclination for life, in spite of the fact that he was only nine years old.

Having to drag all that extra weight around meant that George's ageing joints were creaking, and he was taking very little exercise. Whereas previously he had been quite an active cat, he now spent much of his time sleeping in his basket on the floor, showing little enthusiasm for anything other than moving back and forth to his food bowl.

It was only when his owner took him to the vet because she was worried about the difficulty that George was having in walking that she became aware of the extent of his weight problem and how it was affecting his quality of life. She followed the vet's advice about slimming George down and soon noted that he had started to become more lively.

The thing that pleased her most was when George started jumping up readily on to the sofa again to sit with her in the evenings. Previously she'd had to lift him out of his basket and place him alongside her. Although his joints were obviously suffering from the effects of ageing, it had proved possible, by reducing the amount of weight that they had to support, to ensure that George regained his mobility and playful nature once again.

his obesity fuelled by a daily diet of some 2.7 kg (6 lb) of pork and chicken.

Since the risk of obesity increases as your cat ages, so it is important to persuade your pet to eat a formulated food, even if in the past, you have tended to use home-cooked food. Formulated food has the additional advantage of containing key ingredients, such as antioxidants, which will help to offset the effects of the aging process. Their calorie content will also be more in keeping with the needs of an older cat. If you adhere to the recommended guidelines when using this type of food, then you should have no worry about your cat putting on weight again as he becomes older, or if he is already in the senior age bracket.

Walking Your Cat

Of course dog-walking is generally accepted as a means of exercising canine pets, but few people consider taking their cat for a walk. Cats can, however, be trained to go for a walk on a leash and this can provide them with exercise if it is not safe or possible for them to roam outside freely.

It is much easier to teach a cat to walk on a leash from kittenhood. Older cats often resent being constrained in this way and are likely to react by rolling around on the ground, trying to break free, snarling and attempting to scratch you if you try to pick them up. Special harnesses for cats are available from many pet stores, and you must first accustom your cat to wearing one. Only once it is used to wearing the harness should you attempt to attach the leash. Keep the harness on your pet for relatively short periods at first, starting at about five minutes and then increasing this to 10 minutes, depending on how it reacts. Some breeds, notably Siamese and other Orientals are much easier to exercise in this way than others, such as Maine Coons, which tend to have a more independent nature.

When you attach the leash, try to prevent your cat from becoming distressed by stroking and reassuring it. Gradually, your cat will learn that it can move easily, despite being restrained. Before attempting to leave home, try walking alongside a wall, keeping the cat in the middle, as this makes it much harder for him to pull away, and will encourage him to walk in a straight line next to you. Once you have achieved this, you can take your cat outdoors and repeat the exercise.

Your priority when taking your cat outside, and especially in busy or built up areas, should be to make sure that your pet does not become scared or stressed. Avoid places where you are likely to

encounter vehicles or dogs at close quarters. If you make the experience pleasurable, your cat will be more willing to repeat the exercise and will hopefully begin to enjoy these outdoor excursions.

Cats can adapt surprising well to being walked on a leash, but make sure they are used to the leash and harness before you take them outdoors.

Incentives to Stay Slim

Competitions, shows and even races can all provide a great incentive to make sure your cat reaches and stays at its target weight. Enrolling your cat in an event will force you to focus your attention on your pet, maintain your motivation, and will act as an incentive to reach and maintain an ideal weight. It can also be a good way of increasing the bond between you, or other family members and your pet.

Cat Shows

Even if your cat is not a pedigree breed, you can still enter it into a show. There are classes for non-pedigrees at many events, with the cats divided into classes according to the length of their coat – long- or short-haired.

You can find details about shows in the cat magazines, as well as on the internet. It is important to make sure that you enter in time, carefully completing the entry form and returning this with the appropriate entry fee to the show secretary. In the days leading up to the show, you need to concentrate on ensuring that your cat is in the peak of condition, so that he will make a favourable impression on the judges.

Non-pedigree cats are judged on the condition of their coat and their friendliness – a good incentive to improve your cat's overall health and fitness.

There is a key difference between the judging of pure-bred classes and other cats as there are very specific judging standards laid down for each breed. They relate to specific aspects of the cat's appearance, such as the shape of its head, for example, and its coloration or markings. These are allotted specific points, with the cats in a class being judged not against each other, but rather against what is considered to be the 'ideal', as reflected by the judging standard. This is why it is much more difficult to win awards in pedigree categories – there is no standardization of this type for other cats.

Grooming

Judges of other cats concentrate largely on the cat's condition, as well as its degree of friendliness. If you want to win the class therefore, your cat must be in peak condition. It is also vital that you groom your pet very carefully, so that it looks at its best. There is normally no need to give your cat a bath before a show. Washing your cat's coat can even be counterproductive, especially if it is long-haired, because the hair will lose its attractive gloss and shape. Some of the techniques used by those exhibiting pedigree cats, however, can be useful when you are preparing your own household pet for a show.

If you want to clean your cat's coat, then you may want to consider giving your pet a bran bath (beware though, it is a messy procedure!). Bran can be purchased from most pet shops. First, you need to warm it slightly in the oven. Then place your cat at a convenient height on a table and rub the bran thoroughly into its coat; this will help to

absorb excess grease. You can then brush and comb the coat thoroughly to remove all traces of the bran. It is best to do this a couple of days or so before the show.

On the day of the show, having groomed your cat's coat carefully, you can use a piece of silk in the case of a short-haired cat, to brush its coat in the direction of the lie of the fur. This will

Even preparing a long-haired cat for a show is unlikely to be any more complex than its normal grooming routine, entailing careful brushing and combing.

emphasise the gloss. Also make sure that your cat's eyes are clean, with no trace of tear staining in the corners near the nose. This should be wiped away with damp cottonwool.

Check your cat's teeth and ears are clean and check whether its claws need trimming back. If your cat was particularly obese, there may be some folds of skin hanging down on its belly; these should not count against him, if he is now healthy and well groomed.

When you set off to the show, do not forget to take a brush and comb with you to give the finishing touches to your cat's appearance. It is also vital to take your cat's vaccination certificates and the entry details, which you will have been sent. Aim to give yourself plenty of time to arrive at the show, so that your pet will be able to settle down before judging takes place. If your cat is still upset from the journey it may be aggressive towards the judges and end up being disqualified!

You may be surprised – your new slim-line companion may catch the judge's eye and emerge as a winner! You may even come home with a trophy, as well as a rosette.

Top Cat

You will usually have to leave your pet while judging takes place. This heightens the excitement of the event, while allowing the judges to concentrate on assessing the entries, rather than being distracted by the owners. You may find that your newly slimmed down cat attracts the attention of the judge and ends up walking away with the trophy!

One of the exciting things about showing pet cats is that the results often tend to be less predictable than the classes for pedigree cats, simply because there are no precise judging standards. It often depends very much on how your cat reacts on the day, and whether it catches the judge's eye. Hopefully though, even if your cat is not amongst the winning entries, you will both have had a good day out, and the extra fun and preparation involved will help to motivate you to ensure that your pet does not slip back into bad habits and obesity. Shows should be treated as a fun activity, which would have been impossible to attend when your cat was overweight. A show also provides a great opportunity to meet fellow feline enthusiasts from whom you may acquire advice as well as encouragement to continue your pet's new healthy regime.

Cat Racing?

Although dogs ranging from terriers and Huskies to Greyhounds participate in various forms of racing, attempts to establish similar events for cats have proved largely unsuccessful, although this has not deterred people from trying. The earliest appears to have been an informal race held in Liège, Belgium, each year as part of the carnival celebrations during the 1850s. People released their cats at a set spot, from sacks, with the first cat home being declared the winner. On one notable occasion, the race was actually won by a blind cat.

During the 20th century, there have been more organized attempts to encourage cat racing on similar lines to Greyhound racing, with the electric hare being replaced by a mouse. One of the first racetracks for this purpose was set up in 1936 at Portisham, Dorset, and extended over a distance of 202 m (220 yds). Perhaps unsurprisingly, the cats refused to join in this spectacle, although this doesn't seem to have deterred another attempt in 1949 in the county of Kent.

While it may be possible to encourage your cat to take walks (see page 124), or even compete in an agility competition (see page 130), it is therefore very unlikely that you will be able to interest it in racing for exercise. Still, it provides an interesting insight into what cats can and cannot be encouraged to do by their owners.

Cat Agility Competitions

Cat agility competitions have proved to be more successful than cat races. They are often held at cat shows, notably in North America, where the first one was held in 1983. There is now an international organization promoting this activity. The course typically calls for a fenced-off area of 6 x 6 m (20 x 20 ft), with draping around the base of the barrier. This encourages the cats to concentrate on the course, rather than being distracted by whatever is going on elsewhere in the show arena.

A number of different items can be incorporated into the course design, including hoops, tables, enclosed tunnels, ramps, jumps and weave stations, also known as slaloms. Any type of cat can take part, but they must be at least 8 months of age. All cats start at the novice level, with the course being smaller in this case than at the advanced or expert levels. The course is designed to ensure that the cat goes around it in an anticlockwise direction. The handler stays in the ring to offer encouragement, but cannot touch the cat with their hands at

any stage, to steer or otherwise assist it around the course.

The length of time that a cat takes to complete the course is combined with the number of faults to determine the winner. A cat that achieves a flawless performance but has a slow time around the course will beat a cat with a superior time but a number of faults, although there is a maximum time-limit of three minutes. If a cat refuses to complete one of the elements on the course more than once, a fault is awarded. A cat can have two attempts in a competition, and only the best performance is counted. Although no particular breed appears to be better at agility than others, male cats do seem to score more highly than females. This may be related to their natural instinct to wander and explore farther afield.

If you want to enter your cat into an agility competition, you will need to train your pet first. Visit some events or watch them

Your cat will become increasingly agile again once it has lost weight, and this will be especially apparent outdoors.

OUTDOOR AGILITY

If you have access to a garden, you may be able to set up a training course there. Try to ensure that the garden is as secure as possible, and reinforce the fencing if necessary, to deter your cat from straying. This may entail putting netting on gates, for example, and checking for any gaps in the fencing. If you do not feel that it is safe to allow your cat outside to exercise, you could construct a special outdoor cattery (see page 132) where your pet can play when you are out. Put some agility items into the cattery

A log, or some wooden planks arranged to create a balancing exercise or run, can encourage your cat to practise simple agility techniques.

for your cat to practise on. Local suppliers of agility equipment may be hard to find, but suitable items can easily be bought over the Internet.

on the Internet, so that you can see what is involved. You can then purchase the basics to build your own course at home. Even if you do not want to take part in competitions, allowing your cat to exercise in this way will be beneficial, helping to use up calories and ensure that your pet remains fit.

You will probably find it easier to teach the different components of the course one by one, and then combine them together, keeping the sessions relatively short. Some owners use clickers as a way of encouraging cats to learn agility routines. Instead of rewarding the cat with a food treat every time that it achieves what is required, the owner squeezes the clicker. The sound of the clicker indicates to the cat that it has responded as required, and reinforces the newly learned routine in the cat's mind. Do not give your cat a food treat every time that you click. Not only may your cat regain weight if you do so, but your pet can easily become conditioned to expect the treat, rather than focusing on what you are teaching. It is much more effective just to give your cat an occasional treat; the hope but uncertainty of being rewarded in this way should have the result of encouraging your pet to concentrate. Cats learn much more effectively this way.

Building a Cattery

If you are worried about allowing your cat to roam, but want to provide a long-term solution to your cat getting outdoor exercise and have sufficient space, you could build a cattery. This will keep your cat safe during the day while still providing plenty of space for exercise, and you can then bring your pet indoors when you come home at night. With heating incorporated into the shelter, there will be no risk of your cat becoming chilled on a cold day. If your cat has always been kept in the home, however, wait until spring when the weather is warmer before transferring your pet to an outdoor cattery.

Cats are likely to become bored indoors, simply staring out of the window. By having a well-equipped cattery in the garden where your cat can can play safely, the likelihood is that he will exercise more in these surroundings.

Basic Design

You can buy catteries as sectional units that simply need to be assembled on a suitable base. Although individual designs vary, a cattery is generally rectangular in shape and typically comprises an outer run made of wire mesh panels, measuring at least 2.7 m long, 0.9 m wide and 1.8 m high (9 x 3 x 6 ft), with a snug, inner sleeping area approximately 0.9sq m and 1.8 m high (3sq ft x 6 ft); this means that you will be able to walk inside with little, if any, need to bend down. Catteries are often advertised in cat magazines, and some firms will deliver and erect the structure for you.

If you decide to build a cattery yourself, construct the run from timber that is at least 37 mm (1.5 in) square. Use the timber to build frames of the required dimensions and then clad the frames in 16 G (16-gauge) mesh. Make sure that there are no sharp ends of wire mesh accessible to your pet – cover the ends of the wire with battening, if necessary. The mesh must always be attached to the timber with special netting staples rather than ordinary staples from a staple gun, so that there is no risk of it becoming loose and creating a gap through which your cat might escape. This is especially likely if your pet decides to climb up the mesh at any stage, because the cat's weight may pull ordinary staples out of the framework.

The inner shelter should be built in the form of a shed, with at least one window on the side, but not located in a position that will be in direct sunlight when the sun is at its hottest around midday, as this could cause the interior to become uncomfortably hot. Another window may be set in the door as well.

Entry Points

It is sensible to have a safety porch comprising two doors, so that your cat cannot slip past you and disappear when you enter the cattery. This porch should measure about 0.9sq m (3sq ft), with an outer door hinged so that it opens outwards and an inner door that opens inwards. You will also need an interior door within the cattery to connect the shelter and the run. The interior door should be hinged to open outwards from the shelter, into the larger area provided by the run. A cat flap can be positioned on this door, allowing your cat to move in and out of the shelter easily.

GARDEN FEATURE

If you are worried that the cattery will be an eyesore in your garden, try to landscape it into a garden feature, such as a pergola with roses. Make sure that if you grow plants adjacent to the mesh they will not be harmful if nibbled by your pet. Climbers can be trained up the side of the shelter on trelliswork, but avoid growing these plants up the mesh itself, because their weight is likely to weaken the structure as they grow larger. The external timber finish can also be painted or stained to blend in with the surroundings; there are some attractive green and blue colours now available.

Siting and Regulations

When deciding where to site the cattery, try to find a level area of ground that is free from trees, because this will make construction easier. It also helps to choose a location relatively near your home, so that you do not have too far to go to attend to your pet's needs. This will also make it easier for an electrician to run an electrical supply there from your home.

Always check in advance whether you need any form of official permission before starting to build an outdoor cattery, or you could find that you have to demolish or move the structure at a later stage.

The situation is likely to be more complicated if you are living in a rented property, although the cattery itself will not be a permanent brick-built structure.

Footings and Flooring

The cattery needs to be supported on blockwork footings, extending below ground for about 30 cm (12 in) and a similar distance above ground. Mark out the borders accurately with a line, ensuring that everything is properly aligned before constructing the footings. Also make sure that you include a row of blockwork to support the front of

Make sure that the floor of your cattery, or any space where your cat is confined, is hygienic and can be easily cleaned. Linoleum or tiles make a good surface.

best option may be to use concrete paving slabs. These can be hosed off easily and are not as permanent as a concrete base, although concrete can be used if you prefer.

A drainage hole at an appropriate height needs to be set at the lowest point in the surrounding blockwork to ensure that water entering the cattery will drain away readily, rather than pooling on the floor. This is important because there will be times when you will want to scrub over the floor and rainwater will need to drain away. You may want to employ expert help for this task, to ensure that the floor is level and will drain well, whether you are using concrete or paving slabs.

Roofing Concerns

It is easier to construct a sloping roof rather than an apex design for the inner shelter. Make sure that the roof is angled so that it is higher at the front than the back, carrying rainwater away from the run. The roof needs to be robust, so heavy-duty marine plywood is a better choice than boarding.

Roofing felt makes the most suitable covering on the roof of the shelter, and it will pay to use the most expensive grade. The first part of the outside run should also be partially covered, so that your cat is not exposed to the worst of the weather whenever it ventures out from the shelter. Clear plastic sheeting can be attached on to the sides of

the inner shelter as well as footings for the external porch. Try to avoid preparing the footings when the weather is very hot or frosty, because this may affect the ability of the mortar to dry properly.

It is a good idea to prepare the flooring for the cattery at this stage rather than when the walls are in place. You can leave the base of the cattery with an earth floor, but this is not very hygienic. Also, when it rains, your cat will become muddy, so the

the run nearest to the shelter, extending out from the shelter for about 1.2 m (4 ft).

Plastic sheeting can also be used on the roof of the run adjacent to the shelter, corresponding to the extent of the sheeting on the sides of the structure. In this case, opaque sheeting may be a better option, affording more protection against direct sunlight. Guttering will also be needed along the rear of the shelter's roof. Do not allow

A snug, dry shelter area with somewhere where your cat can sleep during the day is an essential part of the design of a cattery, even though you will want to bring your pet in at night.

water to pour down into the run, because this will create unpleasant conditions for your cat. It is often surprising just how much water can flood down during a heavy spell of rain into the run, and if the outflow is blocked, by leaves for example, the base can easily become flooded.

Internal Considerations

It is important to design the inner shelter of the cattery so that it provides a snug retreat for your pet when the weather is bad. In temperate areas, insulation is recommended. Suitable insulation quilt can be purchased from DIY outlets, The insulation quilt can be concealed easily behind

FIT FOR THE FUTURE

Even before your cat reaches its target weight, you will begin to notice signs of improvement in your pet's overall health. Whereas in the past, your cat was probably rather inactive, sleeping for long periods and often stirring only when food was on offer, you are likely to see that your pet has become a much more lively and attentive companion as a direct result of losing weight.

Many people find that it is as if their pet has not just shed weight, but years as well, regaining the temperament and playfulness of a younger cat. This may not just be the result of weight loss, but also because you will have been paying more attention to your cat. As a result, the bond between you and your pet will have grown stronger, benefiting you both. Just remember this change if you find yourself slipping back into bad habits with your cat, feeding your pet too much and not playing with it enough – it should be a great incentive to keep your pet fit and healthy for the future.

plywood panelling. Remember that it is not just the sides of the building that are important in terms of heat loss, but also the roof; draft excluders on the doors may also be useful. Effective insulation helps the interior of the shelter remain relatively cool on hot day, as well as warm during the winter.

It may also be useful to have an electrician to fit a power supply to the cattery. You can then incorporate a dull-emitter infra-red lamp, out of the cat's reach, that will provide warmth when the weather is cold. If necessary, you can link this to a time switch. Electrical lighting also makes it easier for you to collect your pet from the cattery if you arrive home after dark. Use a suitable cat carrier to transport your pet indoors, because if you slip for any reason, there will be no risk of your cat running off into the night.

The floor inside the shelter needs to have a solid base of concrete or paving slabs, with either tiles or linoleum applied on top. This will make it simple to mop the floor regularly, which is important because this is where your cat will be provided with its food and water during the day.

Cats enjoy climbing up tree trunks, apart from using them as scratching posts. If you include one in your cattery, or in the garden, you must be certain that it cannot roll over and hurt your cat.

TIPS TO KEEP YOUR CAT SLIM

- Always make sure that there are toys lying around that your cat likes to play with.

- Always try and wake up your cat when you arrive home after being out for long periods.

- Keep to a routine of feeding: this means that it will be harder to mistakenly feed the wrong amount of food to your cat and overfeed him or her.

- Arrange your home and garden with your pet in mind.

- If you notice a change in weight in your pet, try and take action at once, rather than delaying.

- Have fun with your cat: understand they are independent spirits and learn more about cats in the wild in order to appreciate their lifestyle.

- Exercise in short bursts is better than trying to make your cat play for long periods.

- Talk to your cat and respond to him when he comes up to you to encourage him to be more active.

Toys and Activities

It is important to incorporate a wide range of toys and activities in the cattery, both indoors and out, for your cat to play with while you are out during the day. It is easy to construct climbing frames of various types, and create a sleeping area off the ground. It is also a good idea to place a bean bag on the floor beneath the heat lamp, as an alternative area where your cat can sleep.

Suitable toys for inside the shelter include a small lightweight ball that your cat can pat around with its paws. In the run outside, provide your cat with opportunities to climb. Try to utilize the height of the cattery. If you can acquire any tree trunks of reasonable thickness, incorporate them into the overall design so your cat can climb on them, and also use them as scratching posts to keep its claws in trim. Try to plan out the space creatively, to use as much of the run as possible, while still making it easy for you to move around as necessary.

Index

Author's Acknowledgements

Many thanks to everyone at Cassell Illustrated who helped to bring this idea to fruition, and particularly to Anna and Joanne, for making it such an enjoyable project, and for being so committed to it . Also thanks to my daughter Lucinda for her assistance, not forgetting James and Mandy at Watson, Little Ltd for their encouragement too.

Picture Credits

Alamy 27; /Arco Images 51; /Juniors Bildarchiv 6-7, 48, 63, 67, 81, 113, 131, 137; /blickwinkel 127; /Isobel Flynn 7 right, 35, 64; /Robert W. Ginn 33 bottom, 52; /Chris Howes/Wild Places Photography 107; /Neal and Molly Jansen 38; /David Kilpatrick 93; /Martin Paquin 88; /plainpicture/Schneider, R. 122; /Mark Scheuern 136; /Ian Shaw 50; /Bob Shirtz 23; /TBKMedia 6 left, 54; /Konrad Zelazowski 128.// Ardea 89, 120-121, 124-125; /John Daniels 9, 47, 130, 132-133; /Jean Michel Labat 20, 44, 126; /Johan de Meester 75; /Richard Porter 30.// Corbis UK Ltd 91 /Little Blue Wolf Productions 98-99; Empics/Owen Humphreys 97; Frank Lane Picture Agency/ Foto Natura Stock 43, 70; /David Hosking 102; /Mitsuaki Iwago 69; /Gerard Lacz 17, 33 top; /Jurgen & Christine Sohns 83; /Peter Verhoog 15.// Getty Images/Judith Haeusler 2 right, 108; /Neo Vision 134-135.// Octopus Publishing Group Limited/Jane Burton 117; /Steve Gorton 79, 85, 111, 119, 139; /Ray Moller 21, 34; /Ron Sutherland 87.// Photolibrary Group/Ifa Bilderteam 25; /Mauritius Die Bildagentur 57; /Japack Photo Library 105; /Robert Marien 114-115; /Richard Packwood 2 left, 40; /J-C&D. Pratt 58, 60.// PhotoDisc 10-11, 12-13 bottom, 13 top.// RSPCA Photolibrary/Geoff du Feu 68; /E A Janes 73.